Group Exercises For Enhancing Social Skills and Self-Esteem

(Volume 2)

SiriNam S. Khalsa

Professional Resource Press
Sarasota, Florida

Published by Professional Resource Press
(An Imprint of Professional Resource Exchange, Inc.)
Post Office Box 15560
Sarasota, FL 34277-1560

This book was produced in the USA using a patented European binding technology called Otabind. We chose this unique binding because it allows pages to lie flat for photocopying, is stronger than standard bindings for this purpose, and has numerous advantages over spiral-binding (e.g., less chance of damage in shipping, no unsightly spiral marks on photocopies, and a spine you can read when the book is on your bookshelf).

The copy editor for this book was Patricia Rockwood, the managing editor was Debbie Fink, the production coordinator was Laurie Girsch, Bob Lefebvre did the text design and typesetting, and Carol Tornatore designed the cover.

Library of Congress Cataloging-in-Publication Data

Khalsa, SiriNam S., date.
    Group exercises for enhancing social skills and self-esteem (Vol. 2) /
SiriNam S. Khalsa.
       p. cm.
    Includes bibliographical references.
    ISBN: 1-56887-056-6
    1. Social skills--Study and teaching--Activity programs. 2. Self-
esteem--Study and teaching--Activity programs. 3. Group
psychotherapy. I. Title.
HM299.K35 1999   96-11493
158'.1'07--dc20   CIP

ACKNOWLEDGMENTS

This book was written with the purpose of assisting all the dedicated people who continue to help both themselves and others relate in a more mature and caring fashion.

Special thanks to Dr. Larry Ritt and the staff at Professional Resource Press for their editorial and production support in guiding this second book to publication, to my wife Kirn Kaur for her lightness and patience during my long late hours on the computer, to my daughter Ananda and son Dharm Bir Singh, to my caring mother Phyllis Vita and brothers, and to all those who have supported and continue to support my work in leading group exercises. Sincere thank you to Yogi Bahjan, PhD, for his ongoing contributions towards our understanding of human development and excellence. Thanks to Justin Murphy for his illustrations. Special appreciation to Jack Canfield for his support and his devotion toward the upliftment of others.

TABLE OF CONTENTS

FOREWORD

What a delight to come across a solid, well-written, and easily understood book that guides the human resources worker through the pitfalls of the social world. SiriNam Khalsa's book, *Group Exercises for Enhancing Social Skills and Self-Esteem* (Volume 2), is a gem of a book written in a style that is accessible to the professional and the layperson alike. It charts the territory that every child, adolescent, and young adult must map in his or her own journey to maturity and responsibility in the modern world.

The goals SiriNam Khalsa outlines from the very beginning let the reader know the scope and content of this book. The approach is a clear, cognitive-behavioral one in which the gradual exploration of the outer social world with its many ups and downs are mirrored in the inner world of self-esteem, self-image, and all the shifting matrices of an emerging identity. The goals are simple and clearly written. Being successful in that simplicity is the bedrock of how we prosper and thrive in the world of relationships with others, our society, our family, and ourselves.

For the beginner in this area there are clearly articulated roles and skills for the group leader on many projects. For the professional there are new and supplemental ideas to round out a program already in place. It is workable for the inpatient and the outpatient setting, and most definitely a reliable guide to the endless demands placed upon the skilled human services worker.

I found clear sections on working with mild depression, with issues of self-esteem, and that internal critic that holds the young person back from emerging into the full positive light of his or her own identity. Each exercise has not only a discussion, but also a direct application. The worker who uses it will not get lost in the details. In this way it is both a highly structured guide, and at the same time, one that offers flexibility to adopt to one's particular circumstances.

Because of his success with the first book of exercises, the author developed 60 new items for Volume 2. Detailed exercises on teaching the person in need of social skills the nuts and bolts of *how* to ask for help, of *how* to deal with peer pressure, and how to recognize the *real* stress embedded in new social situations is a strong pillar of the book. While some guides offer behavioral changes and others offer psychological understanding, this little gem of a book adds *both* to the mix in a clear, workable approach.

If you are a human services worker looking for a source book for group skills learning or a professional seeking additional techniques for your job, SiriNam Khalsa's book will find a welcome place on your bookshelf.

Edward Bruce Bynum, PhD, ABPP
Director of Behavioral Medicine
University of Massachusetts Health Services
Author of The African Unconscious *and*
    Families and the Interpretation of Dreams
September 1999

PREFACE

It is with enthusiastic support that I write the "Preface" for the second volume of *Group Exercises for Enhancing Social Skills and Self-Esteem.*

As educators, counselors, and people in the helping profession, we have a tremendous responsibility to reach and teach all people who are in need of a healthy self-esteem. SiriNam Khalsa has once again developed a creative collection of group exercises which enhance the foundation for self-esteem growth and social skills awareness.

Today's educators and counselors carry added responsibilities because significant social changes have had an impact on human relationships. Family constellations have shifted toward an increasing amount of single parenting as well as a loosening of family ties. Young people are exposed to influences that tend to foster aggressive behavior and messages that lack guidance based in values that support personal well-being. Consequently, stresses in many families and classrooms are often high.

SiriNam has read the signposts and once again has responded with a practical series of activities designed to aid the experienced as well as beginning group leader in giving help to those in need. I believe this book can assist any professional who works with groups in a variety of settings with the admirable and essential job of helping others gain a greater understanding of themselves and, therefore, others.

Jack Canfield
President of the Foundation for Self-Esteem
Culver City, California
Seminar Leader, Co-Author of the Bestselling
Chicken Soup for the Soul *series and*
Self-Esteem in the Classroom
September 1999

INTRODUCTION

When I decided to compile and publish the activities and therapeutic exercises in my first book, *Group Exercises for Enhancing Social Skills and Self-Esteem*, my goal was to share successful strategies that have been used with a diverse population of children and young adults of various ages who have the basic need of learning and then internalizing appropriate ways to behave around others. The goals of these exercises are to give group members the ability to control a situation by actively participating in and contributing to the social outcome. I understand the need for a flexible, ready-to-use activities program that will support all professionals who work toward actively teaching these goals. The overwhelmingly positive response to my first book inspired me to compile an additional 60 exercises that will continue to assist psychologists, teachers, occupational and recreational therapists, and other group leaders to be more creative and effective in their group work.

These exercises are designed to help a wide range of individuals, including those who display hyperactivity or attention deficit disorder (ADD or ADHD), depression, personality or adjustment disorders, developmental and learning disabilities, and general social skills deficits, to become aware of acceptable social behaviors and develop proficiencies in improving their social skills. These exercises have also been successfully used with regular and special needs middle school-aged children.

The exercises in Volume 2 of *Group Exercises for Enhancing Social Skills and Self-Esteem* encourage the development of the types of prosocial skills that ultimately enhance feelings of well-being, self-empowerment, and ultimately positive self-esteem. These exercises are equally applicable for use in both inpatient and outpatient settings, including mental health facilities, residential and day treatment programs, schools, vocational and life-skill training programs, rehabilitation and chronic care facilities, and so on.

ABOUT THIS BOOK

All of the exercises in this book are designed to stimulate group members to think creatively, expand their minds, explore their values and beliefs, and safely consider change where change is needed for personal growth. The skills that group members can acquire through these exercises should serve them well in their real day-to-day social environment. These basic social skills are the foundation building blocks for healthy human interactions in all settings. The acquisition of these skills can also be very empowering and beneficial to the self-esteem of all group participants.

The exercises in this book will help group leaders accomplish several important tasks with the group participants:

1. Guide participants in *acquiring an awareness* of what is acceptable social behavior. Each exercise includes a discussion of the importance of the concepts presented. These active discussions will aid in helping participants increase their knowledge and understanding of appropriate behaviors in a prosocial fashion.
2. Provide participants with opportunities for hands-on *practice* of new social skills in a nonthreatening environment.

Based on many years experience leading social skills training groups, I have found that in order for individuals to actually consider changing their behaviors, they need both the *awareness* of appropriate social behaviors and opportunities to *practice* new behavioral alternatives. Only when both elements are present will they learn to *use* their new skills in a personally satisfying and socially appropriate manner. Intellectual understanding of appropriate behaviors is not sufficient; individuals must also practice performing the new behaviors until they find a behavioral style that is comfortable and rewarding (both personally and socially).

Therefore, one of the tasks for the group leader is the active and deliberate teaching of desirable behaviors on both cognitive and behavioral levels. The leader will also find that these exercises will help group members develop a sense of group connectedness and cooperation. Less verbally expressive members of the group will also be motivated to more actively participate in the group process and will begin to feel more competent and positive as a result of their participation.

ENHANCING SELF-ESTEEM

As will be described below, a primary goal for therapists, teachers, and group leaders is to increase the self-esteem of group participants. This book presents direct, uncomplicated, and nonthreatening exercises to advance that goal.

WHAT IS SELF-ESTEEM?

Before we can identify low self-esteem, we need to understand what self-esteem is. We hear the word a lot these days, but what is it really? How is self-esteem enhanced or eroded in school, at work, in a family system, and during social interactions in the community? What is the relationship between self-esteem and antisocial behavior? What is the role of self-esteem in assisting group members to become what Abraham Maslow called the "self-actualized person" and the "fully human person"? (Maslow, 1962).

Self-esteem affects virtually every facet of our life. Self-esteem refers to how highly we value ourselves. It comes from collective thoughts, feelings, and experiences we have had and continue to have about ourselves throughout life. Self-esteem has been defined by the National Association for Self-Esteem as follows: *"Self-esteem is the experience of being capable of managing life's challenges and being worthy of happiness"* (1995). People who feel good about themselves usually express their feelings in their behavior as well as in an openness to learn and grow from life's lessons. They are more able to meet and solve the problems, stresses, and responsibilities of life with confidence.

SIGNS OF LOW SELF-ESTEEM

People can manifest low self-esteem in many ways. They may not even be aware that they do not feel good about themselves, though they know something is wrong.

A pioneer in self-esteem research, Nathaniel Branden (1969), explains it this way:

Consider that if an individual felt inadequate to face the challenges of life, if an individual lacked fundamental self-trust, confidence in his or her mind, we would recognize the presence of a self-esteem deficiency, no matter what other assets he or she possessed. Or if an individual lacked a basic sense of self-respect, or felt undeserving of love, unentitled to happiness, fearful of asserting thoughts, feelings or needs—again we would recognize a self-esteem deficiency, no matter what other positive attributes he or she exhibited. (p. 22)

Some common signs of low self-esteem are whining, needing to win, cheating in games, perfectionism, and exaggerated bragging; resorting to numerous attention-getting behaviors such as clowning, acting overly silly, teasing, complaining, and exhibiting both verbal and physical aggression; being self-critical, overpleasing, criticism avoidant, withdrawn, blaming, always apologizing, and fearful of success and new experiences; over- and underreacting, being unable to make choices or solve problems; expressing a narrow range of emotions and feelings, demeaning one's own talents, avoiding anxiety-provoking situations, and exhibiting antisocial behaviors.

Dealing directly with group members' self-esteem to promote healthy, socially accepted behaviors as opposed to using external punishers and reinforcers is analogous to curing illness by treating the cause rather than providing temporary relief by treating the symptoms. The exercises in this book can assist the group leader as well as empower group participants to directly promote self-esteem and prosocial skills. In a controlled study in three school districts (Reasoner, 1992), the use of a self-esteem program based on systematic training was found to significantly reduce the incidence of antisocial behavior in schools.

When people exhibit poor social skills and low self-esteem, the process of regaining their self-confidence to change behaviors and attitudes takes time. With consistent focus, the group leader can create opportunities for all group members to get in touch with their own potency and feel comfortable in their group environment as well as in themselves. The second volume of *Group Exercises for Enhancing Social Skills and Self-Esteem* can help people give up negative self-messages and develop positive ones.

GENERAL GUIDELINES

This book provides the group leader with a series of structured exercises that promote dynamic positive group interactions and learning experiences. Most exercises are accompanied by an activity sheet which will serve as the catalyst for group discussions and interactions. Step-by-step instructions for the group are also included with each exercise. This format enables the group leader to "teach to the objective" in a way that is not only easier and more efficient in terms of effort and time, but also fulfills prevailing clinical and educational needs for accountability.

The following suggestions should be considered when using these exercises:

1. Before beginning each group session, identify your goals for that session, select appropriate exercises to further those goals, and review the instructions for those exercises. Make sure you have sufficient quantities of all required materials to conduct the exercises; the necessary materials are listed at the beginning of each exercise.
2. State the purpose of each exercise before it begins. This will focus both the leader and the group on the goals for the session and will help participants understand the benefits of active participation. If group members regard an exercise as meaningful in their lives, they are far more likely to be active participants who learn from the experience.

3. The description of each exercise acts as a basic road map that will assist the leader in "teaching to the objective." Each group discussion description provides in-depth directions on how the leader can promote verbal interaction, skill enhancement, and group cooperation.

4. The leader may periodically want to modify an exercise to insure that it more effectively addresses the needs of group members. Many of the exercises include suggestions for possible variations and adaptations.

5. In my experience, understanding and acceptance of the concept of diversity can best be accomplished by forming groups in which group members represent a wide range of abilities, interests, aptitudes, and backgrounds. Such heterogeneous grouping is preferred while simultaneously attempting to form a homogeneous group with respect to shared social skill deficits.

6. Participants learn best when they have an emotional investment in what is being taught. For that reason, many of the exercises in this book are "open ended" in a way that permits the leader to encourage participants to attach personal experiences, thoughts, and emotions to them.

A FEW WORDS ABOUT COOPERATIVE LEARNING

Dishon and Wilson O'Leary (1994) present a *cooperative learning* model that increases the effectiveness of the learning environment when teaching academic and social skills, as well as democratic values.

The therapeutic exercises presented in this book adhere to the basic principles of *cooperative learning models:*

1. *Heterogeneous Grouping.* The most effective groups are varied in terms of social background, cognitive skill levels, gender, and physical capabilities. The group is randomly formed or selected by the group leader to insure heterogeneity.

2. *Social Skills Acquisition.* Social skills or the ability to work cooperatively are learned skills that can be directly taught. As group participants practice the skill-building exercises, discuss the process, and observe the group interactions, they learn cooperative social skills.

Although group leaders can effectively use the exercises in this book without extensive training in group process or the concepts of cooperative learning, references are included for those readers who may want to learn more about the principles and implementation of cooperative group strategies.

YOUR ROLE AS GROUP LEADER

The group leader needs to:

1. Diagnose and understand the needs of group members including their social skill deficits and dimensions of their self-esteem.

2. Introduce exercises and facilitate meaningful group activities and discussion. It is essential that the leader be adequately prepared for each group session. This includes thoughtful consideration of the goals for the session, needs of group mem-

bers, and how to teach to the objective, as well as preparation for leading the group in the specific exercises chosen for the session.

3. Know when to observe and when to guide the group process.

4. Facilitate discussion with both large and small groups.

5. Adapt the content and process of each session and each exercise to the specific needs of the group and the members of the group.

6. Introduce each exercise in a way that "sets the stage" for the participants and prepares them for the task that follows. It is critically important that all group members understand what they are being asked to do. If some members don't understand, the leader might encourage other group members to help increase their understanding. Such mentoring by group members increases group cohesiveness, cooperation, and the group learning process.

7. Expect to see an increased awareness among group members of their attitudes, beliefs, and feelings. The effective group leader learns to tap into this awareness to help group members increase their self-awareness, sense of self (including self-esteem), and positive behaviors.

Here are some additional thoughts and suggestions for the novice group leader:

1. Choose the setting for the group carefully. When participants are in a comfortable and relaxed environment, they will typically behave in a more relaxed fashion and will be more comfortable in expressing themselves. Consider having group members sit in a circle, because this arrangement promotes eye contact, interaction, and cohesiveness.

2. In general, restrain your urge to fill silence with questions or recounting of personal experiences. It sometimes takes time and a little silent support for group members to collect their thoughts, recall personal experiences, convey their feelings, and think about what they want to say. Be patient.

3. Encourage all group members to participate by making the group a safe and supportive place for all members to express themselves. Establish a climate within the group where all members always have the freedom to respond, or not respond, without fear of judgment, sanction, or pressure from others.

4. Trust is an essential ingredient for furthering human relationships. In order for the group to progress in pursuing the goals and reaching the objectives of these exercises, the group leader must foster the development of a climate of trust in which group members feel genuine caring and empathy.

USING THE EXPRESSIVE ARTS

The exercises in this book rely heavily upon the expressive mediums of writing, drawing, and role playing to facilitate changes in social skills and self-concept. There is a saying: "If you want to know something, read it; if you want to learn something, write it; and if you want to master something, experience and teach it." Teaching social skills and enhancing self-esteem is a process that can be greatly enhanced by encouraging participation in these nonthreatening exercises which promote critical thinking through the expressive mediums of reading and writing, and mastering through role playing and experiencing.

Abraham Maslow identified "learning one's identity" as an essential ingredient for personal change. He stressed that psychoeducation that incorporates the expressive arts "can be a glimpse into one's ultimate values" (Maslow, 1962). In my experience, integrating the use of the expressive arts into social skills training provides nonthreatening modalities for helping group members discover their hidden abilities and increase their sense of self-worth.

The director of the New England Art Therapy Institute, Dale Schwartz, believes that using art as an expressive medium can provide people of all ages and learning styles with concrete images that help them reflect and find the power to change. She also stated that "the use of the expressive arts helps us express feelings and ideas for which we might not have words. It also gives us a safe way to express ourselves" (D. Schwartz, 1995, New England Art Therapy Institute).

When introducing these exercises, remind participants that artistic talent is not important; instead, stress that what is important is the willingness of all group members to freely express themselves. The group leader should also emphasize the noncompetitive and nonjudgmental nature of these exercises and insure compliance with that mandate. Edith Kramer emphasized that "when self-esteem is low, competition does not act as a stimulus; it leads to despair" (1971).

SELECTING EXERCISES

The list below suggests exercises that might be most helpful for the various stages in the group process. It also includes the types and ages of participants that might benefit most from each exercise.

Exercises especially effective for groups in their early stages of development
Exercises 1, 10, 16, 22, 35, 36, 58

Exercises especially effective for groups in their later stages of development
Exercises 2, 3, 5, 7, 13, 14, 17, 19, 23, 24, 27, 30, 31, 32, 34, 39, 40, 42, 45, 46, 47, 49, 50, 52, 53, 54, 59

Exercises especially effective for groups in any stage of development
Exercises 1, 4, 6, 8, 9, 11, 12, 15, 18, 20, 21, 25, 26, 28, 29, 31, 33, 37, 41, 43, 44, 48, 51, 55, 56, 57, 60

Exercises especially effective for groups with participants displaying Hyperactive or Attention Deficit Disorders (ADD or ADHD)
Exercises 4, 5, 6, 10, 11, 15, 17, 18, 20, 21, 22, 26, 31, 32, 35, 37, 38, 44, 51, 58

Exercises especially effective for younger-aged group participants
Exercises 9, 12, 14, 15, 16, 22, 25, 32, 33, 45

RESOURCES

Bean, R. (1992). *The Four Conditions of Self-Esteem.* Santa Cruz, CA: ETR Associates.

Branden, N. (1969). *Psychology of Self-Esteem.* Los Angeles: Bantam Books.

Daley, T. (1984). *Art as Therapy: An Introduction to the Use of Art as a Therapeutic Technique.* New York: Tavistock.

Dishon, D., & Wilson O'Leary, P. (1994). *A Guidebook for Cooperative Learning.* Holmes Beach, FL: Learning Publications.

Goldstein, A. P. (1988). *The Prepared Curriculum: Teaching Prosocial Competencies.* Champaign, IL: Research Press.

Khalsa, S. (1996). *Group Exercises for Enhancing Social Skills and Self-Esteem.* Sarasota, FL: Professional Resource Press.

Khalsa, S. S. (1999). *The Inclusive Classroom: A Practical Guide for Educators.* Glenview, IL: Good Year Books.

Khalsa, S., & Levine, J. (1993). *Talking on Purpose: Practical Skill Development for Effective Communication.* Oceanside, CA: Academic Communication Associates.

Kramer, E. (1971). *Children and Art Therapy.* New York: Schocken Books.

Maslow, A. (1962). *Toward a Psychology of Being.* New York: Van Nostrand.

The National Association for Self-Esteem. (1995). *Self-Esteem Today* (Vol. 8, No. 4). Santa Cruz, CA: Author.

Perls, F. (1971). *Gestalt Therapy Now.* New York: Harper and Row.

Reasoner, R. (1992, April). What's behind self-esteem programs: Truth or trickery? *The School Executive, 1,* 1-20.

Sharan, Y., & Shlomo, S. (1992). *Expanding Cooperative Learning Through Group Investigation.* New York: Teachers College Press, Columbia University.

Yalom, I. D. (1985). *The Theory and Practice of Group Psychotherapy.* New York: Basic Books.

Group Exercises For Enhancing Social Skills and Self-Esteem

(Volume 2)

Being a Good Listener

Purpose:

1. To develop an understanding of careful listening skills.
2. To define what it takes to be a good listener.

Materials:

One copy of "Being a Good Listener" activity sheet for each member; newsprint or chalkboard; writing materials.

Description:

A. The group leader asks a few questions pertaining to things people enjoy listening to.
B. Each participant is asked the question, "Why is it important to be a good listener?" As the group generates reasons statements, all responses, including the leader's, are written on a chalkboard or newsprint.
C. The responses are reviewed by reading each response and discussing its importance.
D. Each participant is asked to pair up with a partner and answer the questions asked on the activity sheet.
E. Members are asked to voluntarily share their answers with the group.

Group Discussion:

- The group leader can ask questions such as: "What are some things people like listening to? A favorite song? Musical instrument? A humorous radio disc jockey? The voice of a close friend calling you on the telephone? The sound of your dog barking welcoming you when you come home? The cheering of fans at a sporting event? There are a lot of things we like to listen to."
- The group leader then explains the importance of being both a good listener and a good speaker to experience social success, but this activity will focus on *how to be a good listener.*
- Reasons for why it's important to listen to other people should include the following:

    ✓ People want to talk about what is on their mind.
    ✓ It makes people feel important to be listened to.
    ✓ You can learn things from others by really listening to what they have to say.

- When discussing the group's answers, members can offer personal examples.
- This exercise can be used with a variety of age groups at all stages of development.

Being a Good Listener

Directions: After reading or having your partner read the story below, fill in the answers to the sentences.

People listen to other people for many reasons. Would you listen to a friend if he or she had a problem? People often want to talk about what is on their mind. It helps if they know someone is really listening. It shows that you really care.

It feels really good when you know someone stops talking to listen to what you have to say. People feel important when you take the time to listen to what they have to say. While you are listening, you may also learn a lot. There are so many interesting things you can learn by really listening. If someone is teaching you something or giving you directions, you have to listen to learn. Have you ever gotten lost because you didn't follow someone's directions? Listening not only can be fun but can save time as well!

WHAT ARE SOME REASONS TO BE A GOOD LISTENER?

1. People talk for many reasons. They want to _____ about what's on their mind.

2. When you listen to someone, it shows that you really _____.

3. People feel _____ when you listen to them.

4. While you listen to someone, you can also _____ about a lot of interesting things.

5. If someone is teaching you something, you must listen to _____.

6. Listening can be fun and also save _____.

Who's a Good Listener?

Purpose:

    1. To gain greater awareness of what entails being a good listener.
    2. To develop group connectiveness around a focused objective.

Materials:

    Copies of the activity sheet "Who's a Good Listener?" for each participant; chalkboard.

Description:

    A. The group leader introduces the activity by telling the group members that they will be asked to first listen to a story about four friends talking and "listening" to each other. Then the members will identify which characters in the story were the good listeners.

    B. After reading the story, the leader will pass out activity sheets to four volunteers who will take a character role and read it out loud while the rest of the group listens again.

    C. The volunteers are then asked to role play the story as if they were really talking to each other. The activity sheet can be used as a guide.

    D. Members are then asked to form small groups of four and take turns answering the discussion questions. After 5-10 minutes the leader will facilitate a discussion of their answers.

Group Discussion:

- When discussing the responses to the discussion questions, the leader explains that it is through the mode of listening that we can learn a lot about people we are interacting with. It's important to state that it may not always be easy—in fact, often difficult—to be quiet and to really concentrate on what someone is saying. But this skill is well worth developing.

- When participants give their responses to the questions asked on the activity sheet, the group leader asks them to find evidence in the story that supports their answer.

- It can be helpful to write down on a chalkboard the answers to the question, "How could Jose's listening have helped Ananda?" Responses can include: Let Ananda get her feelings out, and/or help do some problem solving.

- This exercise is most effective with groups that are beyond the early stage of development and have established some interpersonal communication skills.

Who's a Good Listener?

Directions: After reading and role playing this conversation, discuss the questions below.

ROLE-PLAY 1

Characters: José, David, Ananda, and Tanya—four friends
Setting: Waiting in line at a movie
Goal: Identify the good listener(s)

David: José, Tanya, you guys are late. Where's Ananda?

José: Yeah, I had to wait to get a ride from my sister, and then Tanya wasn't ready when we got to her house!

Tanya: I told you I was on the phone with Ananda and, oh here she comes. Hey, Ananda, what's up? We were wondering if you were going to make it.

Ananda: (*Sadly*) Yeah, I know. My father is having trouble getting around and needs help with stuff like walking up the stairs and putting his coat on. He thinks he might need another operation and that means I'd have to take care of my little brother.

David: (*Sympathetically*) Wow, that sounds like a real drag.

Ananda: It is, and I think. . . .

Tanya: My little sister is a real pain. I can't wait until she gets her own room.

David: Why does your father need an operation?

Ananda: He hurt his back at work and it's not getting any better—

José: My father is always complaining about his health. He smokes a pack of cigarettes a day! Does anyone have a smoke?

Tanya: José, you don't smoke.

José: Just kidding (*turns to Ananda*). Will your father be able to drive us to the party this Saturday?

Ananda: Well, I don't know . . . it depends if—

José: Hey, there's Steve! Let's let him get in line with us (*begins waving his hand to get Steve's attention*).

DISCUSSION QUESTIONS

1. Who do you think were good listeners?

2. Why?

3. How could you tell that José wasn't interested in listening to Ananda?

4. How about Tanya? Did she show good listening skills?

5. What was bothering Ananda? How could her friends' listening have helped her?

6. If you were Ananda, what would you have done in this situation?

Listening to Directions

Purpose:

1. To establish good listening and concentration skills in learning and daily living.
2. To practice effective listening and concentration skills in small groups.

Materials:

One copy of "The Three Cheese Sandwich" activity sheet for each member; writing materials; chalkboard or large paper if chalkboard is not available.

Description:

A. The group leader first establishes the purpose of this exercise by saying, "Listening is one of the most important skills we must learn as children and young adults. Listening will help us to understand directions and solve problems."
B. The group participants are asked to listen while the leader reads the story "Making a Three Cheese Sandwich."
C. The following questions are asked of the group members:

   ✧ "Do you think Kim will be successful in making her sandwich?"
   ✧ "What are some things Kim could have done to show she was really listening to the directions?"

D. After reviewing the different skill components, the members are asked to form several groups of two to role play. Each group is given an activity sheet and is asked to role play Kim taking directions from her supervisor at work. The participants will demonstrate appropriate listening skills. Five to 10 minutes should be given for practicing the role play.
E. The participants who are watching the role play will give feedback as to how well each member fared in listening to directions. Each role play should take 1-2 minutes.

Group Discussion:

- When generating listening skills, the group leader should list the following components on the chalkboard or ask participants to write them down on their activity sheets:

   ✓ When someone is speaking to you be sure to look at them.
   ✓ Really concentrate on what the person is saying.
   ✓ Show you understand what is being said by occasionally nodding your head up and down. This is called positive body language.
   ✓ Take notes if you think you might forget what is being said.
   ✓ Ask questions or repeat what is being said if you're not sure what is being said.

- The group leader should first model the skills being taught by reenacting the making of "The Three Cheese Sandwich." Show the participants how to follow the skill steps.
- Discuss how well the role plays were accomplished and reinforce the skill components.
- This exercise can be very enjoyable but it's not unusual for the first groups who role play appropriate listening skills to make some errors. It may be used best with groups whose members have already established some interpersonal skills.

The Three Cheese Sandwich

Directions: Read the following story. With a partner, identify whether Kim could have been a better listener. Next, with your partner, practice role playing this story by including all the appropriate listening and following direction skills.

Kim is starting her first job at The Special Sandwich Shop. Her new boss, Mrs. Vita, is anticipating a busy day because of a local parade that will be soon coming through town. She wants to teach Kim how to make one of the most popular sandwiches they sell called "The Three Cheese Sandwich."

These are the instructions that Mrs. Vita gave Kim: "Now, Kim, as people order a Three Cheese Sandwich I will ask you to make them in the back room. You start with cutting a 6-inch bun in half, then you spread mustard and our special sauce on each side of the bun. Then add two slices of swiss, muenster, and cheddar cheese on the bun. Next put some onions on top with a slice of lettuce, tomato, and four pickles."

"Oh, at the end remember to add salt, pepper, and some oil and vinegar. Any questions? No? OK, here they come, so let's get going!"

Kim was feeling good that she was given so much responsibility the first day on the job. She really wanted to do a good job. As the first customer ordered, she began trying to make her first Three Cheese Sandwich.

GOOD LISTENING AND FOLLOWING DIRECTION SKILLS

1. _____

2. _____

3. _____

4. _____

5. _____

Following Directions

Purpose:

1. To gain a greater understanding of why following directions is important.
2. To increase awareness of behavior and consequence.

Materials:

"What Happened?" activity sheet for each participant; pens or pencils.

Description:

A. The group leader introduces this activity by explaining that everything we do (our behavior) has a consequence and that not following directions can have disturbing consequences.
B. The group participants are then asked to think about this question: "What's following directions all about?"
C. After thinking for a few minutes (in silence), each member is asked to turn to another person and share his or her answer. The leader will then ask for a few volunteers to share their answers with the group.
D. The leader then passes out the activity sheet "What Happened?" and asks each member to work individually or with a partner to complete the activity sheet. The leader walks around the room checking to see if the group members fully understand the directions.

Group Discussion:

- It's important that group members understand that many people need to first think quietly about the question being asked before speaking out loud. Ask the participants to repeat back to their partner what was shared with them before sharing their answer to the question, "What's following directions about?"
- When the activity sheet is completed, the members can share each answer with the whole group. The leader helps members to recognize any personal experiences that relate to the answers.
- This exercise is especially effective with group members who are having difficulty with responsibility issues and dealing with the logical consequences to their behaviors.

What Happened?

Directions: Below are stories about people who *did not* follow directions. Match what they did with what happened to them by writing the correct letter next to the number. (Answers are discussed with group.)

	ANSWERS

_____ 1. Lee was invited to a party. He was too shy to ask how to get there.

A. Grounded

_____ 2. Joseph was asked to mop the floor after dinner. He was in a hurry, so he mopped before dinner. The floor got dirty again during dinner.

B. Burned popcorn

_____ 3. Yolanda didn't listen to the Science assignment and turned it in a day late.

C. One leg longer than the other

_____ 4. Liza didn't hear her Dad say she should be home by 10:00 p.m. She got home at 10:30 p.m.

D. Received a poor grade

_____ 5. Larry was making a table. He read the directions wrong.

E. Had to mop twice

_____ 6. Maria didn't see the sign that said, "No Turn on Red." She turned when the light was red.

F. Got a ticket

_____ 7. Lin was making popcorn. The directions said to put the oil in the pan first. Lin put the popcorn in the pan first.

G. Ruined shirt

_____ 8. Rosa bought a silk shirt. She did not see the directions that said "Hand Wash Only." She put the shirt in the washing machine with the rest of her laundry.

H. Missed party

Asking Questions

Purpose:

1. To recognize the importance of asking questions.
2. To increase assertiveness skills.

Materials:

"Asking Questions" activity sheet for each member; large sheet of poster board; writing materials; crayons; colored pencils and/or markers; scissors; glue.

Description:

A. The group leader asks the participants to think of a time when someone asked them to do something and they did not fully understand what was being asked.
B. After a short discussion pertaining to the question takes place, the leader passes out the activity sheets and group members are asked to raise their hand if they have a question after *silently* reading the directions.
C. After any *questions* are answered, the participants complete the activity sheet .
D. Participants are asked to sit in small groups to share their cartoon strips. After giving the groups 5-10 minutes of sharing time, individual cartoon strips are cut out and glued on a large piece of poster board for display.

Group Discussion:

- The group leader facilitates the first discussion by reminding the participants that it isn't unusual for someone to be hesitant about asking questions out of fear of possibly looking "dumb." They should be reminded that asking questions is a skill that often takes practice to learn and that is what the activity is about.
- After giving the direction to "Read silently and raise your hand if you have a question," the leader should notice which group members have difficulty following this direction. The leader can then ask those members if they did not understand the direction given, if they were not paying full attention, and so on.
- After the individual cartoon strips are displayed together on the poster board, members are asked to share what they've learned from this activity.
- This exercise can take two sessions to complete and works well with established groups.

Asking Questions

Directions: Below are stories about young people who have difficulty asking questions. In each cartoon, fill in what questions the person should ask to help him or her work together to get what they need.

RAVI AND JAI MAKE PLANS

ASKING QUESTIONS

Now you try it. Draw a cartoon below that shows two people. Write in the question that one of them *should* ask.

Listen Carefully—Then Draw*

Purpose:

1. To develop effective skills in listening and following oral directions.
2. To increase self-awareness and group participation.

Materials:

White unlined paper; pencils; rulers (cassette player is optional).

Description:

A. The leader passes out the materials and asks members to sit straight without touching any of the materials in front of them because they will need to listen and follow some important directions.

B. The group leader then says the following: "I am going to give you directions to draw a simple picture. I will repeat the directions one time so it's important to listen very carefully to my directions. It's not important that the measurements are exactly right. Now get ready.

✦ In the middle of your paper, draw a square. It should be about 4 inches long and 4 inches high. *(Repeat the directions.)*

✦ In the middle of your square, draw a smaller square. It should be about 3 inches long and 3 inches high.

✦ Next draw a rectangle that is 6 inches long and 3 inches wide and touches the bottom of the larger square. The rectangle should be centered under the square.

✦ Now in the upper left corner of the rectangle, draw another smaller rectangle about 2 inches long and 1 inch wide. Under this rectangle, draw a small apple with a bite taken out of it.

✦ Next draw another rectangle in the upper right corner, 1 inch long and 1/2 inch wide.

✦ What did you draw? *(Answer: computer.)*

C. The group members are then asked to share their pictures with another member.

Group Discussion:

- Members share their drawings then discuss: (a) Which directions were difficult to follow and why? (b) If the activity was repeated do they think their drawing would be more accurately drawn? If yes or no, why?
- I have also recorded my directions on a small cassette player and played it back as the participants draw. Some group members who have attention problems seem to focus easier when a tape is playing. This also can be discussed as to why it happens to be true.
- This exercise can be used with a variety of groups whose members have basic measuring skills.

---

*NOTE. From *The Inclusive Classroom: A Practical Guide for Educators* (p. 94), by S. S. Khalsa, 1999, Glenview, IL: Good Year Books. Copyright 1999 by Good Year Books, an imprint of Addison-Wesley Educational Publishers, Inc. Used by permission.

How Well Do I Follow Directions?

Purpose:

1. To gain awareness of listening and following direction skills.
2. To work cooperatively for the purpose of mutual support and feedback.

Materials:

"Following Directions Questionnaire" for all group members; pens or pencils.

Description:

A. The group leader explains: "It is important to gain an understanding of how well you follow directions at home, in school, and at work. It's equally as important that we help each other understand what we do well and where we might need some help in improving our listening and following direction skills. This questionnaire will help us reach these goals."

B. The leader passes out the "Following Directions Questionnaire" to members sitting in small groups of two or four. They are asked to answer the questions as honestly as possible. Then they will exchange papers with a partner for their feedback.

C. When each group is finished evaluating their partners' questionnaires, the group leader will give his or her feedback.

D. After completing the exercise, the members will discuss areas of strength and needed improvement.

Group Discussion:

- Group members read each other's answers and check the answers they agree and disagree on. The leader assists each group in nonjudgmental feedback.
- When discussing areas of strength and needed improvement, if possible, an example of each should be given. For example: "Steven, last week during group meeting you were not sure what to do and didn't ask for help. So that's why I think you hardly ever ask questions when you're confused."
- This exercise should precede Exercise 8. It works best in groups whose members have already established some interpersonal skills and trust.

Following Directions Questionnaire

Directions: Read the questionnaire below. Circle the answers that fit you. Then ask your partner to circle the answers that fit you in a different pen or pencil. The last step is asking your group leader or teacher to also circle the answers that fit you. (Your partner and leader may not be able to answer some of the questions.)

1. When making something do you read the directions carefully?

YOU:	MOST OF THE TIME	SOMETIMES	HARDLY EVER
PARTNER:	MOST OF THE TIME	SOMETIMES	HARDLY EVER
LEADER:	MOST OF THE TIME	SOMETIMES	HARDLY EVER

2. Do you listen carefully when directions are given?

YOU:	MOST OF THE TIME	SOMETIMES	HARDLY EVER
PARTNER:	MOST OF THE TIME	SOMETIMES	HARDLY EVER
LEADER:	MOST OF THE TIME	SOMETIMES	HARDLY EVER

3. Do you listen carefully when a friend is talking with you?

YOU:	MOST OF THE TIME	SOMETIMES	HARDLY EVER
PARTNER:	MOST OF THE TIME	SOMETIMES	HARDLY EVER
LEADER:	MOST OF THE TIME	SOMETIMES	HARDLY EVER

4. Do you think about what you're doing so you don't make mistakes?

YOU:	MOST OF THE TIME	SOMETIMES	HARDLY EVER
PARTNER:	MOST OF THE TIME	SOMETIMES	HARDLY EVER
LEADER:	MOST OF THE TIME	SOMETIMES	HARDLY EVER

5. Do you ask questions if you are confused?

YOU:	MOST OF THE TIME	SOMETIMES	HARDLY EVER
PARTNER:	MOST OF THE TIME	SOMETIMES	HARDLY EVER
LEADER:	MOST OF THE TIME	SOMETIMES	HARDLY EVER

Did you have any "SOMETIMES" or "HARDLY EVER" answers to any questions? Those are the areas that you can improve on in following directions.

Listening Improvement Plan

Purpose:

    1. To develop a plan for achieving goals of listening and following directions.
    2. To increase responsibility and self-confidence.

Materials:

    "My Improvement Plan" activity sheet for each member; completed Exercise 7 Activity Sheet "Following Directions Questionnaire"; pens or pencils.

Description:

    A. The leader begins the exercise by asking the group to review their "Following Directions Questionnaire" and take note of the areas needing improvement. The leader then explains: "By now you have an idea of where you should improve in following directions. This activity will help you come up with a plan to make those improvements."
    B. Each group participant is given a "My Improvement Plan" activity sheet and asked to read the directions and the first question quietly as the group leader reads it out loud.
    C. The first question is discussed in the group. When the leader feels that everyone understands the directions, they are asked to answer all the questions. Members share their completed responses in groups of four or in the large group.

Group Discussion:

- When discussing the first question, "Who is going to help you?," brainstorm a list of possible helpers (e.g., parents, siblings, teachers, friends) and then discuss which individuals would be most responsible and give reliable support.
- After all activity sheets are completed, individuals will share their "game plans" with other partners or in the larger group. Nonjudgmental feedback can be solicited from group members. For example: "I think your plan for improvement is good. I also think that you might do poorly in school if you don't improve."
- This activity should follow Exercise 7, "How Well Do I Follow Directions?" and can be reviewed periodically to check for improvement.

My Improvement Plan

Directions: Answer the questions below. After you're satisfied with your answers, fill in your improvement plan.

HOW WILL YOU SUCCEED?

1. Who is going to help you? _____
_____

2. What are you trying to improve? _____
_____

3. How are you going to do it? _____
_____

4. What will happen if you do this? _____
_____

   What will happen if you don't do this?_____
_____

5. How will you know if you achieved your goal(s)? _____
_____

MY PLAN				
Who?	**What?**	**How?**	**What?**	**How Do You Know?**

Matching Good Listening Skills

Purpose:

1. To increase understanding of skills in effective listening and following directions.

Materials:

"Matching Good Listening Skills" activity sheets; pens or pencils.

Description:

A. The leader explains that establishing good listening skills takes time and practice. This exercise will help all participants increase their understanding of what good listening skills look like and then practice good listening techniques.

B. The group members are asked to form several small groups of two. Each group is given an activity sheet.

C. After completing the activity sheets, each group is assigned one or more listening techniques to role play depending on the number of small groups.

Group Discussion:

- After each group role plays their assigned listening technique, the rest of the members choose the technique that was role played. This can be made into a charades-type of activity to add some excitement to the process.
- When the members choose the correct technique being role played, the leader can facilitate a short discussion, asking participants why it's important to use these skills, and what might happen if you don't use the technique being role played.
- This exercise is effective with many age groups at all stages of development.

Matching Good Listening Skills

Directions: Read each of the following listening techniques and find the drawing on the right that shows how to be a good listener. Place the letter of the correct drawing on the line beside the corresponding technique.

_____ 1. Ask questions.

_____ 2. Repeat what the speaker is saying.

_____ 3. Look at the speaker.

_____ 4. Don't interrupt.

_____ 5. Make comments.

Answers: 1 = E, 2 = B, 3 = D, 4 = A, 5 = C.

Starting a Conversation

Purpose:

1. To recognize the importance of being able to start a conversation.
2. To demonstrate through role playing the difference between effective and ineffective use of conversational skills.
3. To increase self-confidence.

Materials:

Copies of the "Starting a Conversation" activity sheet for all group members; chalkboard or large piece of paper if chalkboard is not available; writing materials.

Description:

A. The group leader begins this activity by explaining why learning how to begin a conversation is important at school, at home, and in the community.
B. A list of "How to Start a Conversation" skills as well as how to keep it going is written on the chalkboard.
C. Participants are asked to write down the list on their activity sheet. An example of each skill should be written next to each one. The leader will give an example for the first skill.
D. The leader will then select two group members for each role play on the activity sheet.

Group Discussion:

- The list of "How to Start a Conversation" skills should include the following:

  ✓ Always greet the other person with a smile and/or handshake and say your name if you've never met before.
  ✓ Establish eye contact with the person you're talking with.
  ✓ Keep the conversation interesting.
  ✓ Ask questions and allow the other person to express himself or herself.
  ✓ Listen to what the other person has to say.

- If any group members are reluctant to write down the skills due to a writing disability, they can instead have a partner write them down while they give a verbal example. The goal is to check for understanding of the list of skills.

Starting a Conversation

Directions: Please copy the list of "How to Start a Conversation" skills. Next to each statement write an example of the skill (number one is done for you). Your group leader will then ask you to role play one of the situations.

HOW TO START A CONVERSATION

1. Always greet the other person with a smile and/or handshake and say your name if you've never met before.

   EXAMPLE: "Hi, my name is Gus. Do you know where. . . ?"

2. _____
   _____

   EXAMPLE: _____

3. _____
   _____

   EXAMPLE: _____

4. _____
   _____

   EXAMPLE: _____

5. _____
   _____

   EXAMPLE: _____

ROLE PLAY SITUATIONS

☆   Starting a conversation at a bus stop

☆   Asking for directions to a particular store

☆   Looking for a lost pet

☆   Applying for a job

☆   Asking a friend for his or her phone number

Striking Up a Conversation!

Purpose:

1. To increase understanding of how to initiate a conversation in different situations.
2. To develop interpersonal skills.

Materials:

Copies of "Striking Up a Conversation" activity sheets for all group participants; writing materials; chalkboard or large piece of paper if chalkboard is not available.

Description:

A. The group leader begins this exercise by explaining to the group that there are different ways they can begin a conversation with someone and that we meet people in a variety of situations.
B. The group members are asked to think of different places and situations a conversation can take place. A list of situations is generated and written on the chalkboard for everyone to read.
C. The participants are asked to think of some ways they can strike up a conversation with someone in these situations. After a few examples are discussed, the activity sheet is passed out and discussed when completed.

Group Discussion:

- When the group members are generating their conversation list, examples of possible situations and conversation starters can include the following:

Situations:

✓ Waiting in line at a movie theater; ask if he or she has heard about the movie.
✓ Making a new student feel welcome; ask where he or she moved from.

- Members are asked to copy two situations from the chalkboard that are not on their activity sheet. After everyone completes their activity sheet, group participants can take turns sharing their answers. Using role play can be an effective strategy to support learning these skills.
- This exercise can be effective with any group and may be used during all stages of group development.
- After each role play the group can discuss the appropriate and inappropriate behaviors and then reenact role play with corrections. Reinforce correct behavior with verbal praise and group reinforcement.
- This exercise is best used after the group's initial stages of development.

Striking Up a Conversation!

Directions: First fill in some ways you can strike up a conversation with someone in these situations. Then copy two situations from the chalkboard that you might find to be a little difficult. Write down some ways to begin a conversation for these new situations as well.

1. Waiting in the dentist's office while someone is sitting next to you

   _____

   _____

2. Being introduced to your friend's parents

   _____

   _____

3. Meeting a neighbor at the grocery store

   _____

   _____

4. _____

   _____

5. _____

   _____

My Helpers

Purpose:

1. To help identify people who could be of help in a problem situation.
2. To increase assertiveness skills.

Materials:

One copy of "Who Are My Helpers?" activity sheet for each member; writing materials.

Description:

A. The leader begins this exercise with these questions: "Think of someone in your life that you would ask for help if you were trying to solve a problem. Would there be more than one person or different people for different types of problems? Why might you choose this person?"
B. The leader facilitates a short group discussion around the attributes one might need to be a good helper.
C. As the activity sheet "Who Are My Helpers?" is being passed out, the group participants are asked to think carefully why certain people might be better helpers for different situations and why that may be true.
D. Volunteers are asked to share their answers and discuss why these people were chosen.

Group Discussion:

- When each member identifies their helpers, they should be encouraged to discuss why they chose these people and in which type of situations they would be most helpful.
- Members should also discuss the different attributes they think make a good helper. For example: someone who is experienced, available to give help, trustworthy, sincere, and/or supportive.
- This exercise can be successfully used at all stages of the group development. It should precede Exercise 13, "Asking for Help."

Who Are My Helpers?

Directions: Make a list of people who could help you when you have a question or a problem to solve. Next to each name write a few positive attributes or things you like about each person. When finished, share your answers with the group.

<u>**NAMES**</u>   <u>**ATTRIBUTES**</u>

EXAMPLE

1. ___My older sister Dina___   ___She's a really good listener___

                                                       ___Knows a lot about people___

                                                       _____

1. _____   _____

                                                       _____

                                                       _____

2. _____   _____

                                                       _____

                                                       _____

3. _____   _____

                                                       _____

                                                       _____

4. _____   _____

                                                       _____

                                                       _____

Asking for Help

Purpose:

1. To learn to ask for help.
2. To increase problem-solving skills and self-confidence in challenging situations.

Materials:

"Asking for Help" activity sheet for each member; writing materials; chalkboard.

Description:

A. The leader describes this exercise as one that will help each participant learn (a) when they need help, (b) who to ask for help, (c) how to use their suggestions, and (d) whether the suggestions worked. These steps are written on the chalkboard.

B. All participants are asked to form teams of three. One of the three members is the "director" whose responsibility is to help direct each role play so the objective is clearly expressed to other group members.

C. Each team receives one "Asking for Help" activity sheet. Participants are asked to read the directions and begin rehearsing one of the role play scenarios.

D. The leader asks for volunteers to role play their scenario for the larger group.

Group Discussion:

- The leader will ask each member to follow the suggested skills for asking for help that are written on the chalkboard:

  ✓ Decide if you need help. If so, what might happen if you don't ask for it?
  ✓ Who should you ask for help?
  ✓ Follow through on their suggestions.
  ✓ Did the suggestions work?

- After each volunteer group role plays their scenario, the group members are asked to critique not only how the role players focused on the skills but also how well the group members critiqued the role play situation.

- In conclusion, the leader will point out that people who learn to ask for help when needed will not feel inadequate. They will feel more confident and become more skillful in their ability to solve personal problems.

- This exercise is most effective with groups that are beyond the early stages of development and should precede Exercise 14, "How Do You Feel?"

Asking for Help

Directions: First copy the four skills needed to ask for help from the chalk-board. Then list two situations when you needed help. Using the skill components as a guide, practice role playing the situations with your partner.

1. The four skills for asking for help are:

   A. _____

   B. _____

   C. _____

   D. _____

2. Two situations when I needed help are:

   A. _____

   B. _____

Now complete these sentences with one of the situations you chose to role play.

1. I really need help when _____.

2. I chose _____ to help me with this problem.

3. These are the suggestions I decided to follow:

   A. _____

   B. _____

   C. _____

How Do You Feel?

Purpose:

    1. To encourage self-disclosure and one-on-one interaction in a nonthreatening manner.
    2. To increase awareness of "feeling words."

Materials:

One copy of "Feeling Words" activity sheet for each member; writing materials; chalkboard or newsprint if chalkboard is not available.

Description:

    A. The group leader begins by explaining the purpose of the exercise, stressing that there are no right or wrong answers to this activity.
    B. The word "Feelings" is written on the chalkboard. Group members are asked to name a feeling they had during the day. A few of these feeling words are written on the chalkboard. The leader explains that we have many feelings during the day and that some feelings are enjoyable and some are not.
    C. The participants sit in pairs answering the questions on the "Feeling Words" activity sheet. When finished, volunteers are asked to share some of their answers with the large group.

Group Discussion:

- The group leader explains that before you can change a feeling, you must first identify and express what it is. When you are in tune with your feelings, you can change if you so desire.
- This exercise can be difficult for those members who tend to deny having different feelings. Referring back to Exercise 13, "Asking for Help," the participants are reminded of the importance of finding someone who will listen as they talk about their feelings.
- This exercise works best with an established group that has developed connections among themselves.

Feeling Words

Directions: If you are working with a partner, take turns reading each feeling word. After each word, take turns writing a sentence describing a situation in which you experienced this feeling.

— *EXAMPLE* —

Feeling word: **confused**

Sentence: I was **confused** after listening to your directions.

---

1. **happy** _____

_____

2. **excited** _____

_____

3. **embarrassed** _____

_____

4. **worried** _____

_____

5. **proud** _____

_____

6. **frustrated** _____

_____

7. **grateful** _____

_____

Thought or Feeling?

Purpose:

1. To make distinctions between thoughts and feelings.
2. To practice empathizing with others.

Materials:

Chalkboard or newsprint if chalkboard is not available; felt-tip marker.

Description:

A. The group leader discusses the purpose of the exercise and then divides the large group into groups of three or four. The participants are told that there will be four rounds of communication, each lasting about 5 minutes each.

B. *First Round:* The leader writes on the chalkboard the phrase "Now I see." He or she explains that during this round participants are to describe the nonverbal behavior of the other members of their group by statements that begin with the phrase "Now I see." The leader illustrates briefly by describing the movements of one of the participants. (A few minutes of processing within the small groups follows each round.)

C. *Second Round:* The leader writes the phrase "Now I think" on the chalkboard or newsprint and instructs participants to continue their conversation, beginning each sentence with the phrase "Now I think." An example is given for the participants' understanding.

D. *Third Round:* In the third phase, the participants are to use "Now I feel." The same procedure as the preceding rounds is followed. The leader suggests two phrases to avoid in this round: "I feel that. . . ." and "I feel like. . . ." Instead, members are to use the phrase "Now I feel" followed by an adjective or feeling word.

E. *Fourth Round:* The fourth phrase, "Now I think you feel," is written on the chalkboard. The participants are instructed to use this phrase at the beginning of their communication with the other members during this round.

Group Discussion:

- Because round four focuses on empathetic understanding, the conversations are two-way, to determine the accuracy of the members' perception of each others' feelings. This round takes 10 minutes, with about 3 minutes processing.
- The leader may have to interrupt if participants begin to move away from the expected behavior and start discussions on what occurred. Give positive verbal and nonverbal praise (smile, pat on the back).
- At the end of the rounds the leader facilitates a discussion of the results of the experience, focusing on the learning goals. The question "What is the difference between a thought and a feeling?" should be asked and discussed.
- This exercise can evolve into the sharing of why people feel certain ways, and is useful with a variety of age groups.

Different Feelings

Purpose:

1. To develop a better understanding of what causes different feelings.
2. To identify feelings of self and others.

Materials:

Copies of the activity sheet "Different Feelings"; pens or pencils.

Description:

A. This exercise is introduced with a short role play by the group leader. He or she begins walking around the room, stomping his or her feet with a scowl on his or her face. Then the group leader asks the question: "What do you think I'm feeling?"
B. Leader distributes the activity sheet "Different Feelings." Participants can work either with a partner or individually.
C. When group participants have completed their activity sheets, the leader asks them to share their answers and discuss the different feelings chosen.

Group Discussion:

- During the discussion of the completed activity sheets, the leader should help members develop a better understanding of their feelings and of others by asking if they have ever demonstrated similar behaviors and the feelings that they experienced.
- Some people would rather work independently when filling out an activity sheet. It's important that they not be given the message that they are not fully participating. These situations can also be brought into the group discussion by asking how participants feel working alone and with partners.
- This exercise works especially well in the beginning stages of the group's formation.

Different Feelings

Directions: Read the behaviors and then think about what that person might be feeling. Pick the word or words from the "Feeling Words" below, and write them on the lines. Remember, there can be more than one correct answer.

FEELING WORDS

1. They stare out a window. _____

2. They are being made fun of. _____

3. They scored a basket. _____

4. They received a good grade. _____

5. They see a dead animal on the road. _____

6. They are laughing. _____

7. They never seem to do anything right. _____

8. They don't ask questions. _____

9. They are crying. _____

10. They are asked to join a team. _____

FEELING WORDS

Happy	Worried	Left Out	Put Down
Fear	Excited	Confused	Frightened
Anger	Bored	Embarrassed	Capable
Sad	Glad	Relieved	Anxious

Expressing My Feelings

Purpose:

1. To increase awareness of different causes and expressions of feelings.
2. To develop an understanding of each other's personal feelings and expressions.

Materials:

One copy of the "Expressing My Feelings" activity sheet; writing materials.

Description:

A. The leader talks about the different feelings people can have during the day and the expression of these feelings by telling this story:

> "It was Saturday morning and Sammy was looking forward with excitement to playing basketball with his friends. He quickly got out of bed, ready to take a shower and get dressed, when he looked out the window and noticed how cloudy it was. It looked like it was going to rain at any moment. Sammy felt disappointed and went back to bed, not to wake up for another 2 hours. He was awakened by the phone ringing. It was his friend José wanting to know why he didn't make it to the ball game. Feeling confused, Sammy again looked out the window and to his surprise it had turned out to be a bright and sunny day!"

B. The leader asks participants to think how Sammy might have felt then and how he might have expressed his feelings.
C. The activity sheet "Expressing My Feelings" is given to each group member to complete. The leader facilitates a discussion of the members' answers when finished.

Group Discussion:

- The follow-up group discussions should include these questions:

  ✓ Why do you think Sammy went back to bed instead of calling his friends?
  ✓ Why do some of you have different causes and expressions of the feelings?
  ✓ Do you think we have a choice in how to feel? How we express our feelings?

- The leader should explain that every person lives by thoughts, and every thought becomes a feeling. What we can begin to understand is how we choose to express these feelings and that this is within our control. Dealing with feelings begins with understanding how we think and then how we choose to react to those feelings we always experience.
- This exercise is effective with all groups that are beyond the early stage of development and have established some interpersonal communication skills.

Expressing My Feelings

Directions: Read the different feelings below. Think of a possible situation that might have *caused* each feeling and write that cause in the second column. Next, think of how *you* might *express* the feeling to others and write it down in the third column.

FEELINGS	CAUSES	EXPRESSIONS
1. Disrespected		
2. Hurt		
3. Joy		
4. Sad		
5. Frightened		
6. Terrific		
7. Worried		
8. Guilty		
9. Grateful		
10. Love		

Quicksand

Purpose:

1. To be able to recognize and *transform* negative feelings.
2. To recognize the importance of not reacting in negative ways.
3. To develop emotional maturity.

Materials:

Chalkboard or newsprint; one copy of the activity sheet "Quicksand Questionnaire" for each group member; writing materials.

Description:

A. The word TRANSFORM is written on the chalkboard or newsprint. The leader asks for a definition and then gives one.
B. The group leader asks this question: "Do you remember a time when you felt depressed or angry and turned it around? Or when you were frustrated, yet you refocused and felt centered?" A short discussion follows with the leader writing on the chalkboard or newsprint any strategies participants used to "turn" their emotions around.
C. The leader then explains that the name of this exercise is "Quicksand" because many people get hooked on the emotional habit of getting angry over small things and taking it everywhere. "Uncontrolled emotion is like *quicksand*. You've got to have at least one foot on the ground in order not to drown in it."
D. The leader passes out the activity sheet "Quicksand Questionnaire." The four steps are first read out loud. The participants then complete the activity sheet, and volunteers are asked to share their answers. Additional strategies are listed on the chalkboard or newsprint.

Group Discussion:

- The word "transform" can be defined as the ability to change from one thing to another. The leader can explain that transforming emotions means being able to change one emotion into another. For example: changing confusion to understanding or boredom to interest.
- One of the most disabling emotions is anger. The leader asks the participants to practice the simple breathing technique of *slowly* counting to 10. This breathing exercise can help participants refocus their mind and calm down angry emotions without sinking. (Refer to Exercise 20 and Exercise 37 for breathing techniques.)
- This exercise is effective with groups in any stage of development.

Quicksand Questionnaire

Directions: Please read the four steps that you can take to *learn from* and *use* to change any painful emotion. Next fill in the statements that will help you understand how these steps can help you not sink in "emotional quicksand."

FOUR STEPS FOR TRANSFORMING EMOTIONS

1. **IDENTIFY WHAT YOU'RE REALLY FEELING.** Feeling anger is usually a surface emotion covering up another deeper feeling like confusion, or not being liked.

2. **WHAT NEEDS TO CHANGE?** Realize that this emotion is telling you that something needs to be changed. Ask yourself, "WHY AM I FEELING THIS WAY?"

3. **REMEMBER A TIME . . . .** Next, think of a time when you successfully handled this emotion and try the same strategy now.

4. **DO IT!** Thinking is just the start. Now you have to change what you are feeling and remember what you've learned so you can do it again and again.

LET'S PRACTICE BY FILLING IN THE SPACES

1. I am feeling _____.

2. This emotion is telling me that I am feeling _____ because

_____

_____.

3. I can remember the time when I handled this feeling by _____

_____.

4. Now I will take some deep breaths and DO IT AGAIN.

> *The key to succeeding with these four steps is*
> *by practicing them and having faith that*
> *you can change how you feel if you try.*

Show and Don't Tell

Purpose:

1. To increase socially acceptable behavior.
2. To gain an awareness of how people can affect others.
3. To increase emotional maturity.

Materials:

One copy of the "Show and Don't Tell" activity sheet for each member; writing materials.

Description:

A. The leader explains the purpose of this exercise by saying: "Even though it's very important to understand what you are feeling and why you feel that way, what you feel and what you *show* others may be two different things. Sometimes it is not acceptable in different social situations to show exactly how we feel."
B. Participants are asked to give a few examples of what the leader has explained.
C. The participants are divided into groups of three or four. Each member is given a copy of the activity sheet "Show and Don't Tell." Participants will discuss why one behavior is more "socially acceptable" than the other.
D. Each small group will be given a situation from their activity sheet to role play for the large group.

Group Discussion:

- When discussing the importance of not always showing what you feel, use yourself as an example. If you are in a bad mood, or something went wrong just before work, or you are distracted by something really good, and so forth, cue your group members in. Demonstrate that even though your feelings go one way, you are controlling what you do—do your job, continue being nice, and so on.
- When the small groups role play their situations, a short follow-up discussion should focus on the ramifications of what each character feels and then what he or she actually shows. The small groups can also role play the consequences of displaying the socially unacceptable behavior(s).
- This exercise works especially well after the group has explored other activities that promote an increased awareness of their feelings.

Show and Don't Tell

Directions: These people have strong feelings about what just happened to them. After reading the situation, read the two possible feeling responses. They showed something different from what they felt. Discuss why the second response is *more* "socially acceptable." Then practice a role play of the two responses for the large group.

THE SITUATION	WHAT HE/SHE FEELS	WHAT IS SHOWN
1. Lucas just beat his friend in a game of basketball.		
2. Maryann got a gift from her grandmother that she knows she will never wear.		
3. José's boss told him that he must get to work a little earlier or find another job.		

(Make up your own situation)   (Draw what the characters might look like)

4.

Anger Control!

Purpose:

1. To increase anger management.
2. To develop effective strategies for releasing stress.

Materials:

Chalkboard or newsprint; writing materials.

Description:

A. Group leader asks participants if they were ever told to count to 10 when they were angry. The leader explains that this is a strategy that many people use to cool down before deciding what to do next.

B. The participants are told that this strategy of counting to 10 works better by incorporating the use of breathing. At this time the leader writes on the chalkboard or newsprint:

> THE BODY IS CONTROLLED BY THE **MIND** AND
> THE MIND IS CONTROLLED BY THE **BREATH**.

C. The leader explains that when the mind is giving angry signals to the body, the use of conscious breathing will change how the mind thinks, from angry feelings to calmer feelings.

D. The group members are asked to practice this strategy together. They are encouraged to try this counting and breathing strategy the next time they become angry and report back to the group on how well it worked for them.

Group Discussion:

- When practicing the strategy with group members, the leader can say the following:

  "When you feel yourself getting angry, try doing the following exercise: Everyone please take a long, deep inhalation and at the same time say the number 1 to yourself. Then relax your entire body as you breathe out. Now inhale and say 2; exhale and relax your body. You're doing great! Repeat the same process on your own continuing with number 3, until you get to 10. I'll observe to see who is following directions."

- The combination of breathing and counting is so relaxing that it's almost impossible to sustain the anger once they are finished. This exercise is also effective in working with stress-related issues.

- This exercise can be successfully used at all stages of the group's development.

Stress Alert!

Purpose:

1. To help plan strategies for handling stressful situations.
2. To increase group support for stress-releasing habits.
3. To increase awareness of stressors.

Materials:

"Stress Alert!" activity sheet for each member; writing materials.

Description:

A. The group leader introduces this exercise by saying: "It's important not to accept a lot of stress in your life. Too much stress can create physical and mental problems. What you want to start doing is noticing your stress early, before it gets out of hand."
B. Group participants are asked to close their eyes and imagine the following: "Imagine that you meet a friend in town and decide to go to lunch together. You look for your wallet and realize it's not where you thought it was. Your body starts to tighten up and you begin to feel panicky. At this point your stress is like a snowball rolling down a hill. It hasn't become too big, so it's manageable and easy to control. However, if you let yourself get really stressed from this incident, the "snowball" will gather momentum and become impossible to stop."
C. The participants are asked to fill out the "Stress Alert!" activity sheet and discuss their answers when finished.

Group Discussion:

- Strategies for stress releasers can include: relax, take a few deep breaths, go for a short walk, talk to a friend, exercise, meditate, think: "What is the worst that could happen?" and "How would I handle it?" and so on.
- During the discussion, each member should be able to express their views on how they would release stress without judgment from others. If an answer involves the use of an illegal drug, the leader can say, "I have found that drugs are a temporary escape from stressful situations and that when its effects wear off one usually finds the stress has increased."
- The leader can end the exercise with this statement: "As you catch your stress before it gets out of hand, you'll find that you'll have far less stress to handle, as well as creative ideas for handling the stress that is left over."
- This exercise is effective with many age groups at all stages of development.

Stress Alert!

Directions: How would you handle these stressful situations? Write the stress releaser after each situation. Write your own stressful situation and stress releaser for number 5.

STRESSFUL SITUATION	STRESS RELEASER

1. You've been waiting all week to watch a favorite TV program and you find out you can't get the channel.

2. You find out that your parents are going to get a divorce.

3. Your best friend has decided to start smoking cigarettes.

4. You're feeling resentful of all the work you have to do with little time to do it.

5. _____

_____

_____

_____

_____

What Is a Friend?

Purpose:

1. To explore what defines friendship within a supportive group environment.
2. To increase awareness of personal values.

Materials:

"Is This a Friend?" activity sheet for each participant; writing materials. Activity Sheet I is for children and Activity Sheet II is for adolescents and young adults.

Description:

A. "The need to belong is very important to a person's positive sense of self, yet many people go through life with few friends. Understanding what a friend is and isn't can be a first step toward developing healthy relationships." The leader shares this with the group, adapting it to the participants' maturity.

B. A copy of the "Is This a Friend?" (Part I or Part II, depending on age) activity sheet is given to each participant to fill out. The focus of this exercise is in the discussion that will follow.

Group Discussion:

- Group members are asked to decide what defines or best describes a friend. The follow-up discussion needs to focus on what describes healthy and realistic relationships and what does not. Reasons that support these concepts should be discussed and debated if necessary. For example, the statement "A friend is someone who doesn't have other friends—only you" should be discussed in the context of possessiveness and jealousy.
- Books on this topic can help participants examine the nature of friendships. (Check your local library or www.amazon.com.)
- This exercise is effective with all age groups in the beginning stages of development.

Is This a Friend?

Part I

Directions: Read the following statements and think about them. Do you agree with the statement? If so circle **YES**. If you don't agree with the statement, circle **NO**. If you are not sure, circle **?**

1. A friend always shares his or her things with you.	YES	NO	?
2. A friend buys gifts for you.	YES	NO	?
3. A friend is someone who sticks up for you.	YES	NO	?
4. A friend is someone who laughs with you.	YES	NO	?
5. Friends always play together.	YES	NO	?
6. A friend is someone who tells you secrets.	YES	NO	?
7. A friend is nice to you.	YES	NO	?
8. A friend says nice things about you.	YES	NO	?
9. Friends never argue.	YES	NO	?
10. A friend never stops being a friend.	YES	NO	?

Is This a Friend?

Part II

Directions: Read the following statements. Circle **YES** if you think it is true or **NO** if you disagree with the statement. If you're undecided, circle **?** Then discuss your answers with the group.

1. A friend is someone who you can always trust.	YES	NO	?
2. A friend is someone who will stick up for you.	YES	NO	?
3. Friends never argue.	YES	NO	?
4. A friend is someone who listens to you.	YES	NO	?
5. A friend is someone you share interests with.	YES	NO	?
6. A friend is someone who would lie for you.	YES	NO	?
7. Friends never disagree.	YES	NO	?
8. Friends never talk behind your back.	YES	NO	?
9. A friend is someone who will always be there for you.	YES	NO	?
10. A friend never stops being a friend.	YES	NO	?

Making New Friends

Purpose:

1. To develop skills to make friends.
2. To create supportive dialogue in a group situation.

Materials:

A copy of "Ways to Make a Friend" activity sheet for each participant; lined paper; pencils, crayons, and other drawing materials.

Description:

A. The group leader introduces this exercise by saying: "Having a friend is a great experience. You can enjoy many things in life together as well as learn from each other. Developing positive social skills can be the key to making friends with someone you like."

B. As the leader passes out the "Ways to Make a Friend" activity sheet and the drawing materials, participants are asked to think of someone they would like to be friends with but have had difficulty in taking the first step.

C. After completing the activity sheet, participants are asked to get together with a partner — someone they would usually not sit with — and share their answers. The group leader can walk around the room and facilitate discussions between partners. If time permits, members can share some of their answers with the large group.

Group Discussion:

- During the discussion between partners, participants should be encouraged to talk about how the different ideas for ways to make friends could apply to their life. For example: "Be assertive when meeting people you'd like to know" can be personalized by inviting someone over your house, joining a club or sports team, and so on.
- If some participants are uncomfortable with drawing, writing a short scenario describing what the idea might look like can be an option.
- This exercise works well with groups who have established some degree of group rapport.

Ways to Make a Friend

Directions: Below are suggestions for ways to make new friends. After reading the idea, draw a picture in the space next to the idea that shows what that suggestion might look like. Then discuss with a partner how these ideas could be applied to you and your life.

SUGGESTIONS	YOUR DRAWINGS

1. Share who you are.

2. Be assertive with people you'd like to know.

3. Don't discriminate based on the person's race, sex, or religion.

4. Smile and introduce yourself.

Establishing Supportive Friendships

Purpose:

1. To explore personal values.
2. To establish positive relationships.

Materials:

"Dealing With Friends" activity sheet for each member; scissors; box.

Descriptions:

A. Many different situations can occur between friends that are not easy to deal with. The leader introduces the exercise by asking members if they have ever been unsure about how to talk to a friend who is doing something that is annoying. Comments from the group are encouraged.
B. The group is divided into pairs. The leader gives each group two scenarios from the "Dealing With Friends" activity sheet. The participants are asked to read each scenario and discuss what they would do in the situation.
C. Volunteers can role play a scenario for the group.
D. *Variation:*

   ✧ The leader gives each pair one scenario to role play.
   ✧ The large group sits in a circle and the scenarios are put in a box in the middle of the circle. Two volunteers pick a scenario and role play for the group how they would respond to the situation. This works best with groups who enjoy role playing. Each role play should last 2-3 minutes.

Group Discussion:

- After the pairs discuss and role play their scenarios, the leader facilitates a discussion focusing on the following questions: "What does your response to the situation tell about how *you* feel about friendships? Is it ever right to end a friendship?"
- Discuss the feelings identified in the role play.
- This exercise works best with older-aged group members who have developed connections among themselves.

Dealing With Friends

Directions: After cutting the scenarios apart, read specific ones and ask yourself, "What would I do if I were in this situation?" Discuss it with a partner and then role play your answer.

SCENARIO 1

Your friend Cara is always forgetting to bring a pencil or pen to school; consequently she is always borrowing yours. One day you're about to take a test and she insists on "borrowing" your pen. It's the only one you have and you'd rather not use a pencil. **What can you do about this?**

SCENARIO 2

Joel has been a close friend for a long time. Lately he seems like he doesn't want to do many fun things together. If you start to hang out with other people, Joel begins to get upset and acts like you've deserted him. You like him but would also like to make new friends as well. **What do you do?**

SCENARIO 3

Ebony is a lot of fun to be with. She is very outgoing and is always thinking of different things to do. Lately she's been wanting to hang out with some people who complain a lot about school, their parents, the police, and life in general. At first these complaints seemed important and you didn't mind listening, but lately it's getting pretty boring to listen to. **What can you do?**

Read My Body

Purpose:

1. To increase understanding of body language and feelings.
2. To develop effective communication skills.

Materials:

Copies of "Body Language" activity sheet for each participant; writing materials.

Description:

A. The group leader introduces this exercise by explaining that we use words to communicate, but it is also possible to communicate without words. This exercise will help in understanding how to "listen" to someone's body language.
B. Copies of the "Body Language" activity sheets are handed out to each group member.
C. When participants have completed their activity sheets, they are asked to form small groups of two to four and take turns sharing their answers.

Group Discussion:

- When participants are completing their activity sheets, the group leader explains that more than one feeling can be perceived and that many kinds of events could have caused each feeling.
- The group explores questions such as "How can reading someone's body language be helpful with friendship?," "Why do you think people sometimes try to hide their feelings?," and "How would you respond to each of the feelings you identified on your activity sheet?"
- This exercise is effective with groups in any stage of development.

Body Language

Directions: Study each face. What feeling is it expressing? Write the feeling and then write two possible causes of the feeling.

FACIAL EXPRESSION	FEELING	CAUSES OF THE FEELING
		1. 2.
		1. 2.
		1. 2.
		1. 2.

Eye Contact*

Purpose:

1. To increase understanding of body language and feelings.
2. To develop effective communication skills.

Materials:

Copies of "Eye Contact" activity sheet for participants; writing materials.

Description:

A. The leader introduces this exercise by explaining that when you are listening and talking to someone, it's important to try to look at the person's eyes. This is called establishing eye contact. Your eyes are windows to how you feel inside. Your eyes change when your feelings change.

B. Each participant is asked to now look at Part I of the "Eye Contact" activity sheet. Participants take turns reading each description out loud. Any comments or questions are discussed.

C. The leader passes out Part II of the "Eye Contact" activity sheet and asks participants to complete it. After this is done, group members are asked to form small groups of two to four and take turns sharing their answers.

Group Discussion:

- This exercise is helpful with group members who exhibit avoidance behaviors. Developing an awareness of eye contact in itself can be a catalyst for profound behavioral change.
- The leader can ask individuals to express their feelings through their eyes and ask the group to try to interpret the feeling being expressed. Questions such as "Why do you think it is important to look into someones's eyes when communicating?" and "Why do some people have difficulty looking at someone when communicating?" should be asked and discussed.
- This exercise is effective with groups in any stage of development.

---

*NOTE. From *Talking on Purpose: Practical Skill Development for Effective Communication* (p. 17), by S. S. Khalsa and J. Levine, 1993, Oceanside, CA: Academic Communication Associates. Copyright 1993 by Academic Communication Associates. Adapted with permission.

Eye Contact

Part I

Directions: Look at these three sets of eyes and notice the difference as you read the descriptions.

Open, direct eye contact

Downcast, teary, pleading,
looking away

Narrowed, cold,
staring but not really "seeing"

Eye Contact

Part II

Directions: Study each pair of eyes. What feelings are they expressing? Write the possible feelings and two causes of the feelings.

EYES	FEELINGS	CAUSES OF THE FEELING
		1. 2.
		1. 2.
		1. 2.
		1. 2.

Pier Pressure

Purpose:

1. To identify the meaning of peer pressure.
2. To develop an understanding of the types of negative pressures peers can feel.
3. To introduce the term self-esteem.

Materials:

Copies of the activity sheet "Pier Pressure" for each participant; writing materials.

Description:

A. The group leader introduces this activity by asking group members this question: "Have your peers or friends ever put pressure on you to do something that you knew you should not do?" After members share their answers, the leader explains that this pressure is called negative peer pressure and that peer pressure can be an uncomfortable experience.
B. The leader holds up the activity sheet "Pier Pressure" for all members to see and asks "Who can identify what this is a picture of?" (answers: a pier, harbor or dock for boats). While holding up the picture, the group leader explains: "This pier has to be strong to resist waves, storms, and ships that push up against it. It has to resist all sorts of pressures to remain standing. People are strong also but are surrounded by pressure to do all sorts of things."
C. Copies of the activity sheet are handed out and the participants are asked to complete the activity and then share their answers with others.

Group Discussion:

- When introducing the exercise, the leader should make clear that a peer is someone their own age; two adults can be peers but never an adult and a child.
- Responses to the different types of peer pressure should include: how to dress, behave, be part of the crowd, use alcohol or drugs, and join gangs. It's important to explain that young people sometimes participate in activities that they know are "wrong" because they want to be considered "cool" by their peers and that nobody wants to be laughed at or rejected by friends for being different.
- After giving the participants enough time to discuss their answers, the leader states the following: "In order to resist these negative peer pressures, you have to be strong enough to withstand the outside pressure or to stand up for yourself. That all starts with a good self-esteem."
- This exercise can be used with a variety of groups whose members have already established some communication skills.

Pier Pressure

Directions: Like the water and boats that push up against this pier, your friends' influence or *peer pressure* can be an uncomfortable experience. In the water surrounding the pier, write a list of possible negative pressures you can feel from peers.

Example:
Skip School

Dealing With Peer Pressure

Purpose:

1. To develop decision-making skills when confronted with peer pressure.
2. To recognize personal values.
3. To increase self-confidence.

Materials:

One copy of the "Role Playing 'NO'" activity sheet for each member; lined paper; writing materials; chalkboard or newsprint.

Description:

A. The leader introduces this exercise by discussing personal values and peer pressure as they relate to antisocial behavior.

B. On the chalkboard or newsprint the leader writes the following list of questions and skill components for dealing with peer pressure:

DEALING WITH PEER PRESSURE

(1) What is most important to me? ▷	Decide what values are most important to you.
(2) What should I do? ▷	Decide what you want to do.
(3) Why should I do it? ▷	Tell the reason for your decision.
(4) Can I stick to my decision? ▷	Practicing saying "no" to the things you really don't want to do.

The participants write down and discuss the different questions and skill components.

C. The group leader models the skill by role playing with a group member the situation, "Several peers are trying to get you to try smoking marijuana." The leader plays the peer being pressured and uses the skill components as a guideline. For example: "My health is more important to me than fitting in. I'm going to tell them that I'm not into taking drugs and stick to my decision. If the pressure becomes too uncomfortable, I'll just leave."

D. The participants are divided into small groups and asked to practice role playing the situations on the activity sheet "Role Playing 'NO.'" Participants then role play situations for the large group.

Group Discussion:

- A value can be defined as a belief or a feeling about something that's important or worthwhile. An example can be someone's belief about eating or not eating meat or recycling paper and cans, and how these values might be an important belief in their life.

- After each role play, reinforce correct behavior, identify inappropriate behaviors, and reenact the role play with corrections. Discuss the role play and how group members were able to avoid negative peer pressure.

- This exercise can take two to three 45-minute sessions. This exercise is effective with any group type, and may be used during all stages of group development.

Role Playing "NO"

Directions: Use the following situations with your group to role play saying "NO" to negative peer pressure. Remember to refer to your "Dealing With Peer Pressure" guidelines.

PEER PRESSURE SITUATIONS

1. Several of your friends attempt to convince you to shoplift.

2. Two peers are trying to get you to cut school.

3. Several peers are trying to persuade you to take drugs.

4. Your friend wants you to sneak into a movie theater with him or her without paying.

5. Your peers pressure you to fight someone they don't like.

6. You're being pressured to join a gang.

Resisting Peer Pressure

Purpose:

1. To develop independent thinking skills to make judgments.
2. To support positive personal values.

Materials:

Drawing paper; writing materials; crayons; colored markers.

Description:

A. The group leader discusses peer pressure in relationship to being able to think independently based on personal values. Saying "No" to negative peer pressure will demonstrate one's ability to distinguish between right and wrong.

B. The leader reads the following story to the group:

"Jason lives in a large city. He's a typical 13-year-old kid who enjoys sports and gets average grades in school. He is liked by his peers and usually stays out of trouble. Recently, he has been troubled by the amount of pressure he's felt to join a community gang. Most of his close friends have been pressured to join a gang. A few of them, like José and Jamal, refused to join. They were harassed and even pushed around while minding their own business. Jason is sure he will be asked to join one of the gangs.

"One day after school while playing basketball at the community park, Jason was approached by a few gang members who have a reputation for being violent. One of the gang members grabbed the ball from Jason and said, 'It's time you show some respect for us and join us or suffer the consequences.'"

C. The group leader asks the group members to listen again while the story is being read and to draw a picture of what Jason might do to resist pressure to join the gang.

D. Participants are asked to share their drawings and discuss the consequences of Jason's decision.

Group Discussion:

- Questions that are asked should include: What should Jason do? What are the consequences? How can he get help from others?
- The leader reminds participants that establishing themselves as a positive, independent thinking person can be difficult at first but feels great over a period of time.
- This exercise is especially effective if it's used before Exercises 53 and 54.

What Is Self-Esteem?

Purpose:

1. To develop a greater understanding of how self-esteem affects your life.
2. To become aware of self-esteem needs.

Materials:

One copy of the "Self-Esteem Questionnaire" activity sheet for participants; chalkboard or newsprint; writing materials.

Description:

A. Group members are asked to give a definition of self-esteem. The leader writes responses on the chalkboard or newsprint. After a short discussion of the responses, the group leader gives this definition of self-esteem: "Self-esteem is our self-worth or how we feel about ourselves. It comes from all the thoughts, feelings, and experiences we have throughout life. It's being able to meet life's challenges and feeling worthy of being happy. One who feels this has high self-esteem."

B. "Self-Esteem Questionnaire" activity sheets are handed out to each group member. In part one, the leader asks participants not to think about each question too long, but to give the first answer that they think of.

C. After the activity sheets are completed, members are asked to pair up and take turns discussing their responses to the questions. After a 15-minute discussion, the group leader collects activity sheets and explains that each member will have an opportunity to meet with him or her to find ways of strengthening areas that are low on the "Self-Esteem Questionnaire" activity sheet.

Group Discussion:

- It's important to remind the participants that this activity is not a test. In part two, there are no "right" or "wrong" answers. This is an opportunity for them to get to know themselves a little better.
- When participants are paired up for discussion, the group leader will circulate throughout the room sitting in on each group to facilitate communication between pairs.
- This exercise works best with an established group that has developed connections among the members.

Self-Esteem Questionnaire

Directions: Read each of the following questions and answer them as honestly as you can.

PART ONE

1. What is self-esteem? _____

   _____

   _____

2. How do you feel and act when you have high self-esteem? _____

   _____

   _____

3. How do you feel and act when you have low self-esteem? _____

   _____

   _____

PART TWO

Circle **YES** if you agree, **NO** if you disagree, and **?** if you are not sure.

1. Do you feel good about yourself?   YES   NO   ?

2. Are you usually glad that you are you instead of someone else?   YES   NO   ?

3. Can you make a list of all your strengths?   YES   NO   ?

4. Are you proud of what you can accomplish?   YES   NO   ?

If you answered "YES" to these questions, you are feeling pretty good about yourself and that shows high self-esteem! If you answered "NO" to any of these questions, then your self-esteem might be low. All this means is that you don't yet KNOW how special you are.

Raising My Self-Esteem

Purpose:

1. To develop specific strategies for raising personal self-esteem.
2. To increase cooperative communication skills.
3. To increase group empathy.

Materials:

One copy of "Ideas for Raising My Self-Esteem" activity sheet for each member; writing materials.

Description:

A. The leader begins this exercise by telling group members that self-esteem is an experience of being worthy of happiness and being able to deal with the basic challenges of life. The leader then facilitates a discussion around this definition of self-esteem.
B. The leader explains that this exercise is about offering suggestions and simple practices that build self-esteem.
C. Participants are asked to form small groups of three or four and discuss the different ideas for raising self-esteem. Each member can take turns explaining the possible benefits of each idea.
D. Group members share which idea(s) they will try and why.
E. *Variation:* The group leader or a member gives each member an idea to practice for raising self-esteem.

Group Discussion:

- The group leader reminds participants to listen to each other's comments about the various ideas on raising self-esteem without interrupting each other or being critical of each other's comments.
- The group leader can return to this exercise throughout the year.
- Participants should be able to practice and discuss the different self-esteem-building ideas for the purpose of clarification and supporting healthy habits.
- I have found this exercise to be effective with a variety of age groups and at various stages of the group's formation.

Ideas for Raising My Self-Esteem

Directions: Read the following ideas for raising your self-esteem. Discuss each suggestion with your group partners. Check one or two ideas you decide to practice during the week.

BUILDING SELF-ESTEEM BY DOING THE FOLLOWING

☐ Learn to ask for what you want.

☐ Before going to sleep at night, think three positive thoughts about yourself.

☐ Look in the mirror first thing every morning and think of three things you like about yourself.

☐ Write down two things you'd like to change about yourself and then do it.

☐ Tell the truth to yourself as well as to others.

☐ Don't associate with people who are negative and complain about everything and anything.

☐ Don't speak ill of anyone or of yourself.

How Do You Feel?

Purpose:

1. To develop an understanding of emotional reactions to different situations.
2. To increase self-awareness.

Materials:

One copy of "How Do You Feel?" activity sheet for each participant; writing materials.

Description:

A. The group leader asks different group members to stand up. Each member is to call out a feeling when pointed to. When finished the leader says: "We have many experiences and thoughts throughout the day which create feelings such as these. Each one of us responds differently to different situations. To help us understand how these feelings can affect our self-esteem, you are going to first fill out this activity sheet."

B. Each participant is handed an activity sheet to complete. After they are finished (10-15 minutes), the participants are asked to discuss the following two questions:

♦ What did you find out about yourself?

♦ What do you need to do more of to feel good about yourself?

Group Discussion:

- After the participants complete the open-ended questions on the activity sheet, ask them to briefly review their answers before beginning the group discussion.
- When discussing the first question, I have found it useful for the participants to give an example or two from the completed sentences that support their answer. If participants answer the second question with one or two words, such as "I need to be nicer, or more confident," ask them to give an example of what "being nice" or "more confident" would be.
- This exercise can be used with a variety of groups whose members have developed some rapport with each other.

How Do You Feel?

Directions: Complete the open-ended sentences below. As a group, discuss the two questions at the bottom of the page.

1. I really like _____

2. I hate it when _____

3. When I feel good, I _____

4. I get embarrassed when _____

5. I'm worried about _____

6. I want to be _____

7. I do best when _____

8. In my free time, I like to _____

9. I need to work harder in _____

10. Someone who means the most to me is _____
    because _____

QUESTIONS TO THINK ABOUT AND DISCUSS

What did you find out about yourself?

What do you need to do more of to feel good about yourself?

Who Am I?

Purpose:

1. To help identify positive and negative traits.
2. To increase understanding of personal values.
3. To explore similarities and differences among group members' values.

Materials:

One copy of the "Who Am I?" activity sheet for each member; writing materials.

Description:

A. The leader introduces the exercise by asking members to define "personal trait." A characteristic or the way someone behaves are good definitions.
B. Members are given a copy of the activity sheet and asked to fill it out individually.
C. When finished, participants sit in a circle and discuss whether the words on the activity sheet are positive or negative and why.

Group Discussion:

- When discussing whether the words are positive or negative, there will be some disagreement. Traits such as "jealous," "quiet," "bored," and "feelings easily hurt" can be both positive or negative depending on the person and circumstance. It's important that group members feel they can disagree and openly discuss their perceptions without being concerned about being judged by their peers.
- Participants can explore similarities and differences with other group members when sharing personal traits.
- This exercise can be used with a variety of groups at all stages of development and age levels.

Who Am I?

Directions: Check off the words below that best describe you. When finished, discuss as a group whether these words are positive or negative.

PERSONAL TRAITS

☐ nice	☐ ugly	☐ underweight
☐ strong	☐ dumb	☐ realistic
☐ bad	☐ sick	☐ alone
☐ weak	☐ handsome	☐ negative
☐ good talker	☐ slow	☐ beautiful
☐ sad	☐ different	☐ masculine
☐ courageous	☐ pretty	☐ feminine
☐ intelligent	☐ angry	☐ responsible
☐ funny	☐ accepted	☐ silly
☐ lonely	☐ shy	☐ good student
☐ street smart	☐ guilty	☐ kind
☐ serious	☐ dull	☐ jealous
☐ well-liked	☐ outgoing	☐ positive
☐ artistic	☐ comfortable	☐ lazy
☐ clumsy	☐ uncomfortable	☐ generous
☐ friendly	☐ talented	☐ ambitious
☐ creative	☐ talkative	☐ hard worker
☐ worried	☐ spiritual	☐ failure
☐ fearful	☐ quiet	☐ _____
☐ athletic	☐ overweight	☐ _____

How many traits checked would you say are:

Positive? _____

Negative? _____

The Critical Inner Voice

Purpose:

1. To change negative mental messages.
2. To enhance self-esteem.
3. To develop group support for self-improvement.

Materials:

One copy of "Changing My Critical Inner Voice," Part I and II, activity sheet for each participant; newsprint; writing materials; crayons; colored pencils; markers.

Description:

A. The group leader introduces this lesson by reviewing the definition of peer pressure and then displays the following statements that have been written on newsprint prior to the group meeting: "In order to resist peer pressure, you have to be strong enough to stand up for yourself. That all starts with having positive SELF-ESTEEM."

B. The leader then defines self-esteem as: "Our sense of self-worth or how we feel about ourselves. It comes from all the thoughts, feelings, and experiences we have about ourselves throughout life. It's being able to meet life's challenges and being worthy of feeling happy." The leader asks questions to check members for understanding.

C. The leader displays these statements that have been written on newsprint and asks group members to *first listen* as the leader reads out loud, then together, read them out loud: "The first step in making self-esteem better is to stop listening to your CRITICAL INNER VOICE. The critical inner voice is the voice inside your head that constantly puts you down. This creates low self-esteem. Everyone has to deal with their critical inner voice."

D. Examples are given of possible critical inner voice messages such as: "I am not smart," or "Nobody likes me." Each member is given activity sheets I and II to fill out. After filling out both activity sheets, group members are asked to pair up for role playing.

Group Discussion:

- This activity takes two 45-minute sessions to complete and then should be reviewed intermittently. Participants should be encouraged to practice talking to their critical inner voices for 1 week and then report back to the group on their progress.
- When addressing the question "Why do we have these negative messages inside our heads?," the Part II activity sheet illustrates one possible reason. The other possible cause that could be discussed is that sometimes it feels comfortable to be critical of ourselves. If we never expect anything good to happen to us, we'll never be disappointed in life. I introduce this concept to teenagers and young adult group members.
- The message group members need to leave with is that they can turn their critical inner voices into allies and that when you believe in yourself, it's easier to say "No" to peer pressure.
- This exercise works best with an established group that has developed connections among the members.

Changing My Critical Inner Voice

Part I

Directions: Answer the following questions:

HOW MUCH DO I UNDERSTAND?

1. What is peer pressure? _____

_____

_____

2. What is self-esteem? _____

_____

_____

3. What is your critical inner voice? _____

_____

_____

4. Why is it necessary to stop listening to your critical inner voice in order to make your self-

esteem better? (Give an example.) _____

_____

_____

_____

_____

Changing My Critical Inner Voice

Part II

Directions: Take time reading the following sections and then answer the questions.

Question: Why do we have a critical inner voice?

Answer: Some people are programmed to think that way from past negative messages that they received when they were younger. Look at the example *Past Negative Message* cartoon:

Question: How do we get rid of our critical inner voice?

Answer: Stop listening to it! Let's start by giving it a name. Every time it speaks to you say its name, then *change* the message you want to hear. For example, you name your critical inner voice the "Terminator" and this is how you can speak to it:

Critical Inner Voice: "You're lazy."

You: O.K., Terminator, I know what you're up to and you're wrong. I help my father around the house, cleaning the yard and putting away stuff.

⇨ Now, give your critical inner voice a name: _____

⇨ Next pair up with a partner and role play having one of you act as your critical inner voice by saying things that are "put downs." For example, "You're stupid" or "You don't stand up for yourself." After each "put down" you respond with a positive self-statement. After four or five messages, change roles, and don't forget to use your critical inner voice's name!

Identity Box*

Purpose:

1. To recognize personal unique qualities.
2. To develop an appreciation of each other's uniqueness.
3. To develop a greater awareness of our public and private selves.

Materials:

Shoe or sneaker box for each member; magazines; personal photographs; glue; scissors; paper; writing materials.

Description:

A. The leader talks about the different things that make someone unique. The group is asked to also give examples.
B. The leader explains that we have a part of ourselves that we show to everyone. We can call this our "public self"; a part that few people know can be called our "private self."
C. Participants are asked to look through magazines and cut out pictures and words that describe their public selves. Personal photos can also be used. These illustrations will be glued to the outside of their boxes and symbolize the part of them that everyone sees and knows.
D. Participants are asked to do the same for the inside of the box, except that these illustrations will show the part of them few people see or know or their private self. Boxes are shared and discussed in the large group when completed.

Group Discussion:

- When the leader is talking about uniqueness, these thoughts should be included: "No one else is exactly like you—you are unique. Part of what makes you unique is the way you express yourself, your likes and dislikes, and your past experiences." Group members can give an example of a unique quality.
- Participants are asked to bring in personal photographs before this exercise. The photos can illustrate home life, pets, family members, and so on. When Diane, the author of this activity, presented it to the group, she used her own identity box as an example which included a photograph of herself on the outside of the box. This photo was taken 15 years ago and represented a special time in her life. The inside of the box, her "private self," had photographs of her family, a personal poem, and other words describing a part of her that few people knew.
- This exercise is a good one to use at the beginning of a group's formation, because it introduces each member in a nonthreatening way.
- See Exercise 36 if participants cannot or do not have a box.

---

*This exercise was inspired by Diane Panico-Mentor, Teacher, Springfield, MA. Reprinted with permission.

Identity Collage

Purpose:

1. To recognize personal unique qualities.
2. To develop an appreciation of each other's uniqueness.
3. To develop a greater awareness of our public and private selves.

Materials:

Colored construction paper; magazines; personal photographs; glue; tape; scissors; paper; writing materials.

Description:

A. The leader talks about the different things that make someone unique. The group is asked to also give examples.
B. The group leader explains that we have a part of ourselves that we show to everyone. We can call this our "public self"; a part few people know can be called our "private self."
C. Participants are given a piece of colored construction paper of their choice. They are asked to fold it in half. The outside flap will have pictures from magazines, words, and photographs that illustrate their "public self." The inside of the folded paper will illustrate their "private self."
D. Materials are handed out and participants are asked to complete their "Identity Collages." When completed, each member shares his or her collage with the group. The collages can then be displayed.

Group Discussion:

- This exercise can be done in place of Exercise 35 or in addition to it if some participants do not have a box.
- Participants can be asked to cut out pictures of people from magazines and bring them to the group prior to this lesson. A bulletin board can be created for this exercise by taping the pictures of all the different people around the edges. The "Identity Collages" can then be stapled to the bulletin board for ongoing display.
- This exercise can be used at the beginning of a group's formation, because it builds a sense of group identity in a nonthreatening way.

Inhale and Relax

Purpose:

1. To develop strategies for handling stress.
2. To increase group support for stress-releasing habits.

Materials:

None

Description:

A. The group leader introduces this exercise by explaining how we all need to take responsibility for our mental and emotional health and that understanding how we can release daily tension is an important step toward personal health.

B. The leader explains that this exercise is another version of the strategy of counting to 10 when someone upsets you. Counting to 10 is used to cool down before deciding what to do next. Saying "inhale" and "relax" directs your mind to tell your body what to do!

C. The leader directs the participants by saying the following:

 ✧ When you feel yourself getting upset, take a long deep inhalation, and as you do, mentally say "inhale."
 ✧ Then slowly exhale and mentally say "relax." Repeat the same process with the number 2, all the way to number 10.

D. Participants are asked to practice this strategy individually or in pairs, and to discuss how they feel afterwards.

Group Discussion:

- During the discussion the leader explains that the combination of counting and breathing helps to clear the mind and relax the body. This technique is based on the relationship between the body, mind, and breath which is that *the body is controlled by the mind and the mind is controlled by the breath*. By controlling our mind we can relax our bodies and release tension caused by angry feelings.
- This exercise can also be used when feeling a little anxious or frustrated. After practicing it, often, it can help you from getting frustrated or angry in the first place.
- This exercise is effective with many group types at all stages of development. I have successfully used this exercise with group members who demonstrate depressive and hyperactive disorders.

Self-Control

Purpose:

1. To learn effective strategies for remaining calm under stressful situations.
2. To increase group support for stress-releasing habits.

Materials:

Chalkboard or newsprint; writing materials.

Description:

A. The group leader writes on the chalkboard or newsprint: "What Causes Stress?" Group members are asked to offer examples of situations that can be stressors in their lives. For example: family problems, unsafe neighborhood, fighting with a sibling, moving to a new neighborhood. These examples are written on the chalkboard or newsprint.

B. The group leader explains that by using self-control strategies, people cannot only control their stress level but also decrease it. A lot of self-control will enable one to deal with many problems; little self-control can only help with small problems.

C. The group leader writes these self-control skills on the chalkboard or newsprint:

   ✧ What is causing you to lose your self-control? Define the problem.
   ✧ How are you feeling? Identify your feelings.
   ✧ Who can you talk to about the problem? Discuss the situation.
   ✧ How can you "cool down?" Practice a stress-releasing strategy (slowly count with the breath to 10).
   ✧ Decide on the best solution while staying in control.

D. The group leader leads a discussion on these skills.

E. Two group members are selected to role play a situation involving their self-control. A group discussion follows each role play.

Group Discussion:

- Examples of possible role play situations include the following:

  ✓ One person accidentally bumps into another while walking.
  ✓ You lost something that was borrowed and discuss it with a very upset friend.
  ✓ One person (the passenger) is getting nervous while driving very fast with a friend.

- The group members applaud the role players whenever they use a self-control skill. The participants identify the self-control skills each participant used after each role play.

The Pursuit of Happiness

Purpose:

1. To increase daily habits that support personal happiness.
2. To gain an understanding of what can make people happy.

Materials:

One copy of "Creating Daily Happiness" activity sheet for each participant; writing materials; lined paper or journal books.

Description:

A. The group leader begins this exercise by asking members to think about what sort of activities make them happy. They discuss what makes them feel happy and why.
B. The group leader states: "Happiness is a state of mind. It's a way of thinking about life and the people we know. Happiness is a feeling that grows by developing habits that help us to feel good about ourselves and other people we know."
C. While handing out the "Creating Daily Happiness" activity sheets, the group leader explains that participants will read a list of happiness-creating habits. Then, after some discussion with a partner, they will choose one or two habits to practice for a week and then discuss what effect the new habits had on their ability to feel good about themselves and others.

Group Discussion:

- The leader helps participants to understand the difference between the often-held belief that happiness comes from external objects rather than from creating a positive state of mind. The leader can use the analogy of undertaking a journey with the goal of achieving happiness or a positive state of mind. It cannot be reached instantly, but like any long journey, it is completed step by step, mile by mile.
- Depending on the maturity of the group members, the leader can explain that most people have deeply rooted thinking patterns that make them unhappy. They cannot be banished overnight, but must be identified and replaced bit by bit with positive thinking habits.
- One or two "Happiness Habits" can be practiced for a week at a time, then evaluated for their effectiveness. Participants can keep a journal to support personal awareness of internal changes.
- This exercise can be effective with a variety of groups that have already established some rapport.

Creating Daily Happiness

Directions: Read the following "Happiness Habits" and their explanations. After discussing with a partner what each habit means to you, choose one or two habits you'd like to try for 1 week. After each week, discuss what effect the new habit(s) had on your ability to feel better about yourself and others.

HAPPINESS HABITS

1. *Avoid watching TV before bedtime.*

   Getting prepared for bed and waking up in the morning are psychologically vulnerable times. Watching TV at these times can create upsetting thoughts that stay with you throughout the day or night.

2. *Smile a lot.*

   There is evidence that smiling changes your emotions to pleasant and your thoughts to optimism. It takes 16 facial muscles to smile and 24 to frown!

3. *Exercise every day.*

   Follow a routine of daily physical exercise that creates a sweat. Get some fresh air as often as you can. Try starting a daily 2-mile walking routine.

4. *Be with supportive people.*

   Create and maintain contact with people you enjoy being with at least twice a week. These social contacts will give you time to be yourself and feel supported.

5. *Help others.*

   There is a saying, "Happiness comes from contentment and contentment comes from helping others." The quickest way to happiness is helping someone else feel happy.

6. *Develop an attitude of gratitude.*

   This habit must begin at the moment you get up from bed. In the morning, stop and think of a few things you are grateful for and your entire day will feel more positive.

Learning from Others

Purpose:

1. To develop an understanding of how to increase self-improvement.
2. To learn to effectively deal with stress and frustration.
3. To develop a healthy habit of how to view other peoples' imperfections.

Materials:

One copy of "Journal for Learning from Others" activity sheet for each member; writing materials; chalkboard or newsprint.

Description:

A. The group leader begins this exercise by asking participants to think of the last time someone did something that really bothered them. They describe the situation and why it was a frustrating experience. The leader writes the experiences on the chalkboard or newsprint.
B. The group leader states: "In this activity, you are going to try something that at first is probably unacceptable to you. However, if you give it a try, you might find that it is actually a great way to release frustration and have some fun doing it. When someone in your life does something that bothers you, instead of reacting to it, you're first going to imagine that person as YOUR TEACHER. The people you meet as well as the people you know are all here to teach you something. Your challenge in this exercise is to figure out what the people in your life are trying to teach you."
C. The leader now uses some of the frustrating experiences the members shared to determine the possible lessons being taught. Each "lesson" is written next to the experience.
D. Members are given a copy of the "Journal for Learning from Others" and are asked to write down their first lesson. The journals will be shared during future group discussions.

Group Discussion:

- This exercise can be a lot of fun while being a catalyst for changing one's attitude and perception from "Why are they doing this to me?" to "What might I learn from this experience?"
- The journal discussions should be nonjudgmental but open for different interpretations of the possible lessons being taught. For example, if a member says that her little brother was whining about not being able to get what he wanted, the possible lessons could include compassion: how difficult it is being 2 years old and not being able to fully communicate your needs. Someone else might suggest that another lesson might be learning a little more about being patient. Having younger siblings is an excellent opportunity to change habits of reaction that often lead to arguments.
- This exercise is effective with groups that have developed adequate communication skills.

Journal for Learning from Others

Directions: This journal is to be used for writing down frustrating experiences you've had with people you meet throughout the day and imagining that each person is actually trying to "teach you something." Possible lessons can include being more patient, tolerant, or understanding, or less judgmental of others' differences. Discuss your experiences and lessons with your group.

> *Change your perception from "Why are they doing this?" to*
> *"What are they trying to teach me?"*

EXPERIENCES   ## LESSON

EXAMPLE

Standing in line at a grocery store; the cashier seems to be going very slow.	Instead of getting upset and frustrated, the lesson is to break my habit of feeling impatient.

Letting Go of Negative Thoughts

Purpose:

1. To recognize and let go of negative self-defeating thoughts.
2. To increase a sense of personal power.

Materials:

One copy of "Letting Go" activity sheet for each participant; paper; writing materials.

Description:

A. The group leader introduces this exercise by telling this story: "There once was a gardener who had difficulty planting beautiful flowers due to the amount of weeds that had seemed to take over the garden. After analyzing the problem, she decided to pull out all the old weeds *before* trying to plant new flowers. After doing this, the garden was fertile ground for the beautiful plants she wanted to grow."

B. The leader explains to the participants that if they are careful gardeners, they can also uproot those old weeds and have a fruitful garden and a flourishing life. The "weeds" are an analogy for the negative thoughts that have been implanted in our minds since we were very young. They get in the way of feeling good about who we are and who we can become in life.

C. The "Letting Go" activity sheets are passed out. Participants are asked to fill out their sheets individually.

D. The group leader facilitates a follow-up discussion on how it felt to "uproot old negative weeds."

Group Discussion:

- This exercise is not based on positive thinking, but on attitudinal change. It is important that the participants understand that by doing this exercise, they may not release all their negatives; it will, however, give them a sense that letting go is possible.

- The group leader leads a discussion on why the process of letting go of old negative self-defeating thoughts can help participants begin to take charge of their lives. The discussion should not focus on what each participant wrote but on the importance of letting go of the negative thoughts and then implanting positive ones in their place.

- This exercise works best with groups whose members are insightful and beyond early stages of development.

Letting Go

Directions: Write down all your *negative thoughts* about each subject listed below. Use other pieces of paper if necessary. When you feel you have really cleared out your mind, crumple up the papers and throw them away! Understand that these negative thoughts are like *garbage* and can be thrown away.

SUBJECTS TO WRITE ABOUT

1. Life

2. My Body

3. School or Work

4. Relationships (Family and Friends)

5. Love

Seeds of Positive Thoughts

Purpose:

1. To replace negative self-defeating thoughts with positive ones.
2. To develop healthy thinking habits.

Materials:

One copy of "Changing My Thinking" activity sheet for each member; writing materials.

Description:

A. The leader asks the group members to think back as far as they can to when they were very young. Volunteers are asked to share their memories with the group.
B. After 5-10 minutes of sharing, the leader asks the participants to think of a negative thought that seems to stay in their mind, and then asks the question, "How old do you think you were when this thought was planted in your mind?"
C. Group members are given a copy of the "Changing My Thinking" activity sheet and are asked to read the directions quietly as the leader reads them out loud. After clarifying any questions about the activity, participants are asked to sit by themselves and begin the exercise.
D. Leader facilitates a follow-up discussion emphasizing the importance of taking responsibility for what you think and the consequences of these thoughts.

Group Discussion:

- The leader should introduce information about how our conscious and subconscious minds work by including the following: "The thoughts you dwell on are what you create in life. Positive thoughts get positive results. Thoughts are stored in the subconscious mind. Most thoughts are subconscious, so your results in life are always reflections of your subconscious mind. The more firmly the thought is rooted in your subconscious mind (which is a function of how often you've repeated the thought) the more "real" it seems to you. If you have done "wrong" things in your life, it was a result of "wrong" thinking and vice versa. The purpose of this exercise is to remove negative subconscious thoughts and replace them with empowering ones.
- This exercise should follow Exercise 41—"Letting Go of Negative Thoughts."

Changing My Thinking

Directions: Think of something positive to say about yourself. Write down this thought in the left column. Write it over and over, about 20 times a day. On the right-hand column is your response to the positive thought. Every time you write the positive thought, pause, and write your reaction or the first thought-response that comes to your mind. Then notice it but don't dwell on the response. The responses will vary, and some will not be very supportive. Remember, whatever response comes up is on its way out of your subconscious mind. Also remember to breathe consciously as you write your positive thoughts down.

Examples of Positive Thoughts:

I am fine just the way I am.

I like the way I am no matter what!

I am a good friend to have.

I deserve relationships that are fun and supportive.

NEW POSITIVE THOUGHT	RESPONSES

Affirming Goodness

Purpose:

1. To increase self-esteem and a sense of personal power.
2. To develop healthy thinking habits.
3. To increase ability for dealing with life's challenges.

Materials:

One copy of the "Positive Self-Statements" activity sheet for each participant; drawing paper; crayons; colored markers; writing materials.

Description:

A. The leader introduces this exercise by explaining: "If you say statements over and over, even out loud to yourself, you create positive self-talk in your mind, which eventually makes you feel good about yourself. This positive self-talk or self-affirmations can also be listened to on a tape (made by the group members) while you are relaxing or going to sleep at night."

B. Participants are given "Positive Self-Statements" activity sheets and asked to spend 10 to 15 minutes reading the positive self-statements and writing down any comments about each one as well as writing their own positive self-statement.

C. When the activity sheet is completed, the leader facilitates a group discussion.

Group Discussion:

- During the group discussion, the participants are asked to read some of their comments pertaining to each positive self-statement. Personal affirmations can also be shared. Participants are reminded that when they say the positive statements either out loud or silently, *they should see and feel in their mind as if the statement is already true.* Interpretive drawings can be displayed after discussion.
- Participants can practice their personal affirmations for a week and then report back to the group on any positive changes in behavior or thinking that has taken place.
- This exercise is effective with older group members (teens and above) who have developed some ability for personal insight.

Positive Self-Statements

Directions: Read each positive self-statement and the explanation of its meaning. After each statement, write down a personal comment about it in the space provided.

- Choose one or two statements that are especially meaningful to you and write the statement(s) on top of a piece of drawing paper. Illustrate what that positive self-statement means to you.

GOOD THOUGHTS TO THINK ABOUT

I LIKE MYSELF

Being your own best friend is very important. You have to live with yourself not just some of the time but *all of the time*. Why not get to like who you are, the person you are living with all the time—You? It makes life so much easier.

Comments:

I LEARN FROM ALL MY EXPERIENCES, GOOD AND BAD

Life is like going to school. We are here to learn lessons that come from our everyday experiences. Understanding these lessons will enable you to create a life of self-awareness—repeating the things you like and not doing what you don't like.

Comments:

MY BODY IS MY FRIEND

Your physical body is your vehicle, like a car, that takes you through life. If you take care of your body it will feel good and last a long time. The key is balance: balance in what you eat, how much you exercise, work, play, and rest.

Comments:

I CAN CHANGE MANY THINGS I DO NOT LIKE IN MY LIFE

Taking responsibility for finding solutions to problems you are having in your life starts with right thinking. Your mind is a tool that can help you change the things you don't like in your life.

Comments:

I FORGIVE OTHERS WHO HAVE HURT ME

If someone says something that hurts your feelings, many times they're not even aware of it. If they do it intentionally, they don't like who they are. Forgiving people in your mind who have hurt your feelings helps you to feel better and "lighter."

Comments:

My Personal Positive Self-Statement: _____

_____

_____

Revealing Yourself

Purpose:

1. To increase understanding of the importance of revealing things about oneself.
2. To recognize reasons for sharing oneself in a variety of social situations.

Materials:

One copy of "Why Talk about Yourself?" activity sheet for each member; writing materials.

Description:

A. The leader introduces this exercise by sharing something particularly interesting he or she found out about a friend or group member. After sharing the information (e.g., I found out that Steve plays the piano, or Kara's father is an assistant coach for the University basketball team), the leader uses this opportunity to reveal something about himself or herself that may be interesting to group members.

B. Group members are asked to sit in pairs or groups of three and discuss how revealing information about themselves might help them become better friends with someone.

C. Members are given a copy of the activity sheet and asked to fill it out with the members in their group.

D. When finished, participants sit in a circle and two volunteers are asked to role play an example of a reason for revealing things about themselves for the group. The leader initiates discussion around each role play situation.

Group Discussion:

- As members share their thoughts and opinions about revealing themselves to others, the leader encourages members to give personal examples of times they either took a risk and revealed something about themselves or chose not to, and why they made that decision.
- This discussion might lead to the fact that we all carry secrets around with us and may or may not choose to share them with others. The reasons could include a bad memory of the past or an embarrassing moment about something. For whatever reason, it's okay to be selective about what we let others know about ourselves. However, participants need to understand that selectively revealing things about ourselves can build bridges to others.
- This exercise can be effective with all types of groups at different stages of development.

Why Talk about Yourself?

Directions: Below are some good reasons why it is a good social skill to be able to talk about yourself. After reading the reason, give an example of what someone might say that illustrates the reason. Then role play the example for the group.

REASONS FOR REVEALING YOURSELF	EXAMPLES
EXAMPLE: It's polite.	Hi, I'm Kimberly. I wanted to know if you were interested in playing tennis? I love sports and I'd love to learn how to play.
It can help make interesting conversation.	
You can deteremine how you want people to see you.	
If you open up first to someone, they might respond by opening up to you.	

Knowing My Beliefs

Purpose:

1. To recognize personal beliefs.
2. To increase understanding of other group members' beliefs.
3. To further develop a healthy belief system that can guide one through life's decisions.

Materials:

One copy of the "My Beliefs" activity sheet for each member (Part I is for ages 13 and above; Part II is for ages 7 to 12 years old); writing materials.

Description:

A. The group leader asks for a definition of a personal belief and then gives a definition.
B. Participants are asked to share a personal belief that they've followed since they were very young (e.g., no one should take something that's not theirs).
C. Depending on their ages, each member is given an activity sheet and asked to spend 10 to 15 minutes answering questions. If necessary, questions can be read aloud by the leader or each participant.
D. When the activity sheet is completed, the group is divided into small groups. Each group is asked to discuss their responses to the questions.
E. If a participant has difficulty reading, the group leader or a peer partner can read to the member.

Group Discussion:

- The following can be used as a definition of a belief: "A belief is a thought or feeling that something is important and worthwhile. It could be an idea, a course of action, or something you do. A true belief is based on personal choice, and comes up regularly in one's life. You count on beliefs to guide your decisions in life."
- After giving this definition, ask for examples of beliefs and discuss whether they are true beliefs based on this definition.
- The leader guides each group's discussion by encouraging members to identify similarities and differences of expressed personal beliefs.
- This exercise is most effective in groups that have developed a certain degree of mutual trust and openness with each other. Part I of the "My Beliefs" activity sheet is effective with group members 13 years and older. Activity sheet Part II is modified for younger group members age 7 to 12 years.

My Beliefs

Part I

Directions: Read the following statements. Do you agree with some statements? Do you disagree with some? Do you feel you haven't decided what you believe yet? Circle your response to each statement. Then share your answers with others and notice your similarities and differences *without* judging who is right or who is wrong.

1. People with the AIDS virus should not interact with other people. **I Agree   I Disagree   I'm Not Sure**

2. People who smoke should not smoke outside their home. **I Agree   I Disagree   I'm Not Sure**

3. There is no difference between marijuana and alcohol. **I Agree   I Disagree   I'm Not Sure**

4. It's okay to spank children. **I Agree   I Disagree   I'm Not Sure**

5. Newspaper reporters should stay out of peoples' personal lives. **I Agree   I Disagree   I'm Not Sure**

6. God created everything. **I Agree   I Disagree   I'm Not Sure**

7. It's wrong to kill animals. **I Agree   I Disagree   I'm Not Sure**

8. All music is good. **I Agree   I Disagree   I'm Not Sure**

9. People should live together before getting married. **I Agree   I Disagree   I'm Not Sure**

10. Always tell the truth. **I Agree   I Disagree   I'm Not Sure**

My Beliefs

Part II

Directions: Read the following statements. Do you agree with some of them? Do you disagree? Or are you not sure what you think yet? After circling your response to each statement, discuss your answers with your group members. Remember not to get into an argument about who's right and who's wrong. Instead, listen to what each other has to say.

1. Kids should be able to go to bed anytime they want. **I Agree   I Disagree   I'm Not Sure**

2. Parents usually know what is best. **I Agree   I Disagree   I'm Not Sure**

3. If someone tries to hurt my friend, I'll hurt them. **I Agree   I Disagree   I'm Not Sure**

4. School is fun. **I Agree   I Disagree   I'm Not Sure**

5. Animals shouldn't be kept inside. **I Agree   I Disagree   I'm Not Sure**

6. Parents should never get divorced. **I Agree   I Disagree   I'm Not Sure**

7. Children with handicaps should be in regular classrooms. **I Agree   I Disagree   I'm Not Sure**

8. If you get cancer, you will die. **I Agree   I Disagree   I'm Not Sure**

9. Violent movies should be banned. **I Agree   I Disagree   I'm Not Sure**

10. If you exercise and eat healthy food, you'll never get sick. **I Agree   I Disagree   I'm Not Sure**

Heart Transplant

Purpose:

1. To recognize personal beliefs and values.
2. To work cooperatively with others.
3. To increase listening skills.

Materials:

One copy of "Who Will Live?" activity sheet for each small group of participants; writing materials.

Description:

A. The group is divided into small groups of four or five. The leader explains the situation: "Six people need a heart transplant and will most likely die in 2 weeks if it is not performed. However, the doctors are only able to perform *two* operations within that time period." Repeat the description of the situation a few times until all participants understand the problem they are facing.

B. The leader explains that the group members are to assume the role of the doctor who will perform the operation and therefore must make the decision of who will live.

C. Each group is given one copy of the activity sheet, "Who Will Live?" The leader gives the instructions: "*As a group* you now have a half-hour to decide which two of the six people will be given the heart transplant and therefore live."

D. The leader gives 20-, 10-, 5-, and 1-minute warnings and then stops the groups exactly after a half-hour. Each group shares its decisions with the large group. The leader facilitates a group discussion.

Group Discussion:

- When instructions are given, the leader directs the members to not allow themselves to be swayed by pressure from the others in the group and to try to make the best choices possible. On the other hand, if they do not make a choice in a half-hour, then none of the patients will live due to the limited availability of the two hearts. Each group can have a designated note taker to keep track of everyone's comments.
- During the group discussion, these questions can be asked: "How well did you listen to the others in your group? Did you feel pressured into changing your mind? Were you so stubborn that the group could not make a decision? What do your selections say about your beliefs and values?" Some group members may want to write their answers to these questions privately, or they may be discussed in small groups or in the large group.
- This exercise is most effective in groups that have developed a certain degree of mutual trust and openness with each other.

Who Will Live?

Directions: Below are the descriptions of the six people who need a heart transplant within 2 weeks to live. After discussing the descriptions of these people with each member of your group, decide which *two* people will receive the new hearts and why they were chosen to live. Someone in your group can be chosen as the designated note taker.

PEOPLE NEEDING A HEART TRANSPLANT

1. A 17-year-old girl; a high school drop-out; 4 months pregnant.

2. A minister of a large urban congregation; 65 years old.

3. A mentally disabled child; 9 years old.

4. An established artist; homosexual.

5. An olympic athlete; won a silver medal.

6. A math teacher; 55 years old.

NOTES

A Narrow Escape

Purpose:

1. To recognize personal life values.
2. To increase understanding of other group members' values.
3. To increase listening and group decision-making skills.

Materials:

Flashlight.

Description:

A. The group leader asked the participants to sit on the floor in a close circle. (If sitting on the floor is not possible, chairs are an option.) The lights are turned out and shades pulled down. The group leader turns on a flashlight and explains the situation.

B. "While the group is on an outing to explore some nearby caves, you become trapped hundreds of feet below the ground by a cave-in. There is a narrow passageway leading up and out of the spot where you are trapped. Night is coming fast and no one is around for miles to rescue you. Everyone decides to form a straight line and crawl out of the cave. The members nearest to the front of the line will have the best chances for survival."

C. Each group member will give his or her reasons for why they should be near the head of the line. After hearing each other's reasons, the group members will determine the order by which they will leave the cave. As each member talks, he or she holds the flashlight.

Group Discussion:

- The leader will instruct group members to take turns giving their reasons for why they feel they should be near the front of the line. Reasons should include what they want to live for or what they have yet to contribute to the world that would justify their being nearer to the front of the line.

- Each participant gets a chance to talk and offer their reasons while they hold the flashlight. Members may choose to pass, although this would mean that they would be deciding to allow themselves to be placed near the end of the line.

- This exercise can be very powerful but is most effective in groups that have developed a certain degree of mutual trust and respect among its members.

If You Don't Have a Sense of Humor—
It's Not Funny

Purpose:

1. To increase understanding of the importance of having a sense of humor.
2. To describe how a good sense of humor can affect others.

Materials:

One copy of "Why a Sense of Humor?" activity sheet for each member; a pair of "Groucho Marx" glasses with plastic nose and/or mustache; writing materials.

Description:

A. The group leader begins this exercise by stating: "There is no greater social skill than having a good sense of humor." Members are asked to respond to this statement. After listening to a few comments, the leader explains that seeing the funny side of situations is an important life skill. Someone who can learn to "lighten up" and find humor in events has taken a big step toward getting along with many people.

B. Before continuing, the group leader turns around and puts on the pair of "Groucho Marx" glasses and then faces the group. When the laughing subsides, the leader says: "Someone with a good sense of humor can make a difficult task easy, can make a dull day interesting, and can help others feel better as well."

C. Each participant is given an activity sheet and reads along quietly as the leader reads out loud. Volunteers are asked to answer the questions.

D. The leader facilitates a group discussion focusing on the last three sentences on the activity sheet.

Group Discusion:

- When discussing having a sense of humor, it's important that the members understand what it means to find the "lighter side" of situations.
- Discussion can include making a list of what usually makes people uptight (e.g., being late, being stuck in traffic, not liking the way someone may be looking at you, waiting in line, etc.).
- This exercise is effective in all groups at any stage of development.

Why a Sense of Humor?

Directions: Read the following story of a boy who used his sense of humor to deal with a potentially embarrassing situation. Then answer the questions below.

Josh was really excited about this weekend because he was going out with a group of friends to a movie and then roller skating. He was especially excited about spending time with a girl named Kara because they shared similar interests like sports and movies.

After seeing a movie, the group of friends decided to go roller skating. As Josh was taking off his shoes to put on his skates, he noticed that in his rush to get ready to go out he had put on two different colored socks. It didn't take long before everyone in the group noticed and mentioned it to Josh. He waited for a moment and then said, "Oh yeah, I know. And guess what, I have another pair just like these at home!" Everyone laughed and then proceeded to have fun skating.

A person with a good sense of humor can laugh at himself or herself and consequently cause others to laugh and feel good. Josh might have felt embarrassed but due to his sense of humor, he didn't make the situation such a big deal. His friends enjoyed being around Josh and were able to laugh along with him.

1. Why was Josh excited about the weekend? _____

   _____

   _____

2. What was Josh's potentially embarrassing situation? _____

   _____

   _____

3. What do you think of how Josh dealt with the situation? _____

   _____

   _____

Creating Funny Situations

Purpose:

1. To think of ways in which common situations could be humorous.
2. To develop an understanding of "appropriate humor."

Materials:

One copy of "Creating Funny Situations" activity sheet for each participant; writing materials.

Description:

A. The group leader begins this exercise by sharing a humorous story such as the following:

> "I own a very large dog. He is half Great Dane and half German Shepherd. Last night he was particularly excited about going for his evening walk. The leash I attach to his collar felt like it was stretched to its limit because of his insistence on wanting to run up the street. At one point he began walking around a tree in circles, pulling me along. As I started to become more and more frustrated, a friend of mine saw us and shouted from his car, 'Who's walking who?' Because of his remark, I saw the humor in my situation and consequently relaxed a bit, taking it in stride."

B. The group leader facilitates a short discussion by asking the participants a few questions about the story just told.
C. Each member is given an activity sheet to fill out. They are given a choice to work in pairs and share answers or work independently.
D. Each member is given an opportunity to share a few of his or her answers with the group. Participants who worked in pairs are asked to role play two or three of their humorous situations for the group.

Group Discussion:

- The following questions can be asked during the group discussion: Why do you think my friend shouted out the comment, "Who's walking who?" Was he being rude? Was it an appropriate time to be funny? Why? Has anyone experienced a situation in which a little humor was helpful?
- While listening to and watching the group members share their funny situations, discuss whether any of them are being potentially hurtful in any way and how one can determine what is appropriate humor.
- Ask participants who their favorite comedians are and what makes them funny. Also discuss when it might be a wrong time to be funny (e.g., when someone is trying to share a problem they are having with you, or during a sermon by the church minister).
- This exercise is most effective in groups whose members have developed a certain degree of mutual trust with each other.

Creating Funny Situations

Directions: After reading each situation, think of what could be funny about each one. After writing down your thoughts, if you are working in pairs, role play the situation with a partner. Remember to talk about how something could be humorous without hurting others' feelings.

1. Excuse for being late _____
   _____
   _____

2. Being with a crying baby on a bus or in a car _____
   _____
   _____

3. Going to the dentist _____
   _____
   _____

4. Spilling something at a restaurant _____
   _____
   _____

5. Being afraid of the dark _____
   _____
   _____

6. Visiting relatives _____
   _____
   _____

7. Eating school lunches _____
   _____
   _____

Lighten Up!

Purpose:

    1. To increase understanding of the possible causes of stressful emotions.
    2. To gain awareness of how to change stress-producing thoughts.

Materials:

    One copy of the "Food for Thought" activity sheet for each participant; writing materials.

Description:

    A. The group leader divides the participants into groups of two or three. Each group member is given an activity sheet. The leader asks members to silently read along while the activity sheet is read out loud.
    B. The leader guides each small group in a discussion about the meaning of what was read.
    C. After 10 minutes of small group discussion, one volunteer from each group shares his or her meaning with the large group.
    D. The leader facilitates a group discussion around the exercise.

Group Discussion:

- This is a simple exercise that can have profound results in altering how group members approach life's problems and consequently manage their stress. Remind participants that problems in life will never go away. However, what can change is how we approach or deal with each problem. With practice, our day will feel lighter and more enjoyable.
- During the group discussion, point out that whenever we expect something to be a certain way and it isn't, we become upset and stressed out. Conversely, when we can let go of our rigid expectations and replace them with a preference of the way things can be *and* with an acceptance of the way life is, we feel lighter. Holding on creates stress, letting go is to lighten up.
- Explaining what a "Buddhist" is and how stories are often used to teach a moral or lesson may be needed for some group members.
- This exercise is effective with older age groups who have developed a certain degree of trust and personal insight.

Food for Thought

Directions: First read "A Buddist's View" and "The Story of the Two Monks." Discuss their meanings with others in your group. Next follow the directions for the "Dropping All Expectations Exercise."

A BUDDHIST'S VIEW

In the Buddhist view, what causes tension and stress is the way we think about life, especially when we expect things to be the way we want them to be as opposed to how they really are. Thoughts such as *Why is this happening to me? If only he or she would like me more. If only I could make more money* are not a problem; it's our holding on to them and not accepting what's actually happening that causes us so much stress and frustration.

THE STORY OF THE TWO MONKS

There's an old story that helps to illustrate the point of the Buddhist's view. Two Buddhist monks (or priests) were traveling together when they met a beautiful woman in a silk dress who was having trouble crossing a muddy stream. "I'll help you," said the first monk to the woman, and he carried her in his arms across the stream. The second monk didn't say anything until a few hours later. Then he said, "We monks don't interact with and definitely don't touch females. Why did you do that?" "I left the woman back there," the first monk replied. "Are you still carrying her?"

(Now stop and discuss the point this story is making.)

DROPPING ALL EXPECTATIONS EXERCISE

Try to meet each day *without* expectations. For example, don't expect people to say hello to you. If they don't, you won't be surprised or bothered. If they do, you'll be pleasantly surprised. Don't expect your day to be problem-free. Try instead meeting each problem as another hurdle to cross: "Oh, just another hurdle to overcome." Life will become more of an adventure rather than a struggle or fight. Watch how you begin to lighten up!

Avoiding Fights

Purpose:

1. To recognize what can create an argument.
2. To learn positive ways to avoid getting into fights with others.

Materials:

One copy of the "Alternatives to Fighting" activity sheet for each participant; chalkboard or newsprint; paper and writing materials.

Description:

A. The group leader asks the question, "Why should people consider using alternatives to fighting in order to resolve problems?" and "Does fighting solve problems?"
B. Group members are asked to make a list of the different attitudes and behaviors of people they know who avoid getting into fights. Place a master list on the chalkboard or newsprint and discuss this list with the group.
C. The group leader asks two or three individuals to role play a scenario in which an argument over friendship begins but alternatives to solve the problem are made to avoid a fight.
D. The activity sheet is given to each group participant to fill out and discuss with the group.

Group Discussion:

- The master list of behavioral attributes and attitudes should include the following. Someone who:

  ✓ Asks themselves, "How do I avoid fighting?"
  ✓ Discusses the problem
  ✓ Uses self-control
  ✓ Makes alternative choices
  ✓ Talks to an adult about the incident

- After the role play, group members should critique the role plays by identifying the appropriate and inappropriate responses given by the participants. Different groups of three participants can be selected to role play a similar scenario. Verbal praise should be used for the correct behaviors being role played.
- The group leader points out how different television shows and movies can support these inappropriate fighting behaviors and should be avoided.
- This exercise can be used with a variety of groups at different stages of development.

Alternatives to Fighting

Directions: First fill in the blanks in the following sentences using the words from the "Word Bank." Next, write a short story on the back of this paper of how two or more people avoid getting into a fight by using the alternatives you discussed with the group. The story should include most of the words in the word bank.

```
                         WORD BANK
         choice        argument       adult
         choose        solve          fight
         discuss       self-control   problems
```

1. Fights usually begin with an _____.

2. Does fighting _____ problems?

3. _____ the problem instead of fighting.

4. _____ should be resolved with words and not fists.

5. My friend used his _____ to avoid fighting.

6. _____ another alternative to fighting.

7. Telling an _____ is the mature thing to do.

8. She lost her self-control and got into an awful _____.

9. You always have a _____ whether to fight or not.

Fighting Words

Purpose:

1. To recognize aggressive language.
2. To demonstrate understanding of amiable communication.

Materials:

Poster board (or other large writing surface); markers.

Description:

A. The group leader walks up to a group participant and in an aggressive tone says "Get out of my way!" The leader then pauses and waits for a response. At this point the leader explains that this was a role play and that the language that was used created certain feelings in the group. A short discussion pertaining to those feelings takes place.
B. The group leader asks participants to remember comments they have made that caused their friends or parents to be angry. The participants are asked to repeat the comment in the same tone of voice they used in the original situation.
C. The group members discuss what they could have said in each situation that would have kept the communication amiable.

Group Discussion:

- Examples of comments the group members made that caused others to be angry include:

    ✓ "Give me that. . . !"
    ✓ "I'm going to smack you!"
    ✓ "Shut up!"
    ✓ "Get out of my way!"

- Outline the discussion of the alternatives that would have kept the communication amiable on poster board for easy reference. Role playing the alternatives is an effective option.
- This exercise also can help with understanding the use of appropriate intonation and voice tone.
- This exercise is particularly useful with preadolescents and adolescents.

Talking on Purpose*

Purpose:

1. To identify assertive communication.
2. To develop effective communication skills.

Materials:

One copy of the "Assertive Self-Check" activity sheet for each member; chalkboard or newsprint; writing materials.

Description:

A. The leader writes the words "passive," "aggressive," and "assertive" on the chalkboard or newsprint. Next, the group leader says the following: "The purpose of this activity is to help you communicate more effectively so that you can build friendships, achieve goals, and get more out of life. Let's begin by defining these three ways of communicating."
B. As the leader passes out the activity sheet, the participants are asked to first fill out their sheets individually and then pair up and discuss their answers with a partner.
C. Take turns discussing and role playing ways in which members could become more assertive.

Discussion:

- The group discusses the specific examples on the activity sheet and can either give an example of an alternative assertive response and/or role play the scenario with their partners.
- Definitions for the three words are as follows:

  ✓ *Passive:* Statements that do not communicate what you mean in a direct way.
  ✓ *Aggressive:* Statements that are hostile, attacking, or demanding.
  ✓ *Assertive:* Statements that communicate what you mean and feel.

- When role playing, participants are encouraged to exaggerate the feeling tone and volume of their voices (i.e., passive is low and possibly whiny; aggressive is loud and demanding).
- This exercise is most effective with groups in the later stages of development.

---

*NOTE. From *Talking on Purpose: Practical Skill Development for Effective Communication* (p. 14), by S. S. Khalsa and J. Levine, 1993, Oceanside, CA: Academic Communication Associates. Copyright 1993 by Academic Communication Associates. Adapted with permission.

Assertive Self-Check

Directions: After reading each sentence, write "Yes" or "No" next to each one. Next, discuss ways you could have been more assertive and role play your answer with a partner.

_____ 1. I've eaten food that was given to me that I really didn't like.

_____ 2. I have a difficult time letting people know that I disagree with them.

_____ 3. I'm not sure what to say if I receive a compliment.

_____ 4. I get really upset if someone is angry at me.

_____ 5. I have apologized for something that either I didn't do or wasn't really my fault.

_____ 6. I've done something that was wrong because I felt pressure to do it.

_____ 7. I've worn certain clothing because I wanted to be accepted by friends.

_____ 8. I have a difficult time telling phone solicitors that I don't want what they are trying to sell.

Let's see how you did. Did you answer "Yes" to any questions? These are instances when you found it difficult to communicate assertively. Now practice alternative assertive statements.

Express Yourself*

Purpose:

1. To practice assertive communication.
2. To develop self-confidence in uncomfortable situations.

Materials:

One copy of the "Expressing Disapproval, Concern, and Anger" role play activity sheets (Situations 1, 2, and 3).

Description:

A. The group leader introduces this exercise by explaining how assertive communication can help us deal effectively with difficult situations. Divide the participants into groups of pairs and triads. The triads are given "Situation 1: Expressing Disapproval" or "Situation 3: Expressing Anger." The pairs are given "Situation 2: Expressing Concern."

B. Each group is given 10 minutes to read their situation and practice role playing *assertive* responses.

C. The group leader reads each situation to the group before each pair and triad role play their assertive responses to the large group.

D. The group members discuss the effectiveness of each social interaction after each role play.

Group Discussion:

- In group discussions, be sure to have participants give their *reasons* for their opinions on what is assertive talk. Ask for evidence from the role play that supports what they say.
- When discussing "Situation 2: Expressing Concern," there are many concerns that have to be addressed, such as Alex's desire to be part of the basketball team as well as Michael's desire to keep Alex as a friend. The use of *empathy* in one's communication should also be discussed. How Michael begins his conversation is critical to being empathetic as well as being assertive.
- Find out who your group member's peers are and what pressures are in the member's life. Have volunteers role play assertive responses to some of the difficulties they are experiencing.
- This exercise is especially effective if it follows Exercises 29 and 53.

---

*NOTE. From *Talking on Purpose: Practical Skill Development for Effective Communication* (pp. 42, 43, 45), by S. S. Khalsa and J. Levine, 1993, Oceanside, CA: Academic Communication Associates. Copyright 1993 by Academic Communication Associates. Reprinted with permission.

Expressing Disapproval, Concern, and Anger

Role Playing Situation

Situation 1: Expressing Disapproval

Stacy, Leona, and Cecilia are walking home after school. Stacy suggests that they stop at a convenience store for a snack. Leona tells Stacy that she doesn't have any money. She wants to go in anyway to steal something that she needs. "Let's all go in the store and take something," says Cecilia. Stacy feels uncomfortable about this and wants to tell her friend how she feels.

Role Playing Situation

Situation 2: Expressing Concern

Michael and Alex are good friends. Michael tells Alex he's going to try out for the basketball team. Alex says he wants to try out too. Michael knows that Alex won't make the team and wants to convince him not to try out. He doesn't want to hurt his feelings. Michael is concerned because his friends might make fun of Alex.

Role Playing Situation

Situation 3: Expressing Anger

Lisa and Tai are good friends. They've been taking ballet classes together since they were in second grade. Now that they are in junior high, Lisa's friends want her to spend more time with them after school instead of going to ballet classes. Tai called Lisa a "mama's girl" for taking ballet lessons instead of socializing with her friends. Lisa needs to express anger to Tai and her friends.

Being Successful on the Job

Purpose:

    1. To understand another's point of view.
    2. To make a good impression with your supervisor.
    3. To react appropriately to peer pressure.

Materials:

    One copy of the "Getting Along at Work" activity sheet for each participant; writing materials.

Description:

    A. The group leader introduces this exercise by saying: "When employers are asked why most teenagers fail to keep a job for more than a few months, their answer is because they lack the appropriate on-the-job social skills. This exercise will help you gain some of those on-the-job social skills needed to succeed at work."
    B. Participants are asked to sit with a partner who will help decide the social skills that might be helpful in dealing with the scenarios presented on the activity sheet.
    C. Each participant is given an activity sheet. After filling them out with a partner, they can take turns role playing a situation for the group and discuss each response.

Group Discussion:

- After each role play the group participants should discuss why they chose the particular social skill and if possible give a personal example of the use of the social skill.
- It is helpful to discuss that when employees struggle to get along with their co-workers or their boss, they generally focus most of their attention on the other person. They spend a lot of time and energy thinking about what their bosses do and why they behave the way they do. Discuss why it's equally important to turn the spotlight away from others and put it on themselves. This will help develop the social skills needed to succeed at work.
- This exercise is especially effective with preteen and teenage or older group members.

Getting Along at Work

Directions: After reading each work situation, choose and write a social skill statement from the "Work Word Bank" that might be helpful in dealing with the situation. Next, role play the situation with a partner for the other group members.

WORK SITUATIONS

1. You've been working at the local shopping market for about 2 months and really enjoy stocking the shelves. Your supervisor has changed your job responsibilities to a less desirable one, bagging groceries, and gave your old job to a new employee. When you asked why she decided to do this, her response was that she wanted all employees to be able to learn how to do several different jobs around the store.

   _____

   _____

2. It is Friday and you are looking forward to getting together with some friends after work. Your boss asks you to stay late to help him get things ready for a big sale.

   _____

   _____

3. No one seems to like the new manager who was recently hired. You just heard that some of the employees are planning to call in sick tomorrow so the manager will have a hard time getting things done. They've asked you to join them, but you're not sure if you want to be part of the "call in sick" plan.

   _____

   _____

WORK WORD BANK

Making a good impression.
Responding appropriately to peer pressure.
Understanding another's point of view.

Doing Nothing

Purpose:

1. To increase self-awareness pertaining to on-the-job problem-solving skills.
2. To develop group decision-making skills.

Materials:

Large sheets of newsprint; colored markers; masking tape.

Description:

A. The leader introduces this exercise by saying the following: "Sometimes when people have problems with their boss or co-workers they do nothing about it. In reality this doesn't happen. Nobody really does nothing when they have problems at work. Usually out of fear or not understanding how to take positive-assertive action, people do one or more of the following things." The leader points to four sheets of newsprint taped to different corners of the room with the following different-colored headings written on each one:

   ✧ Complains to somebody other than their supervisor.
   ✧ Keeps the problem inside of them.
   ✧ Does not work that hard.
   ✧ Escapes.

B. After reading each heading and answering any questions, the leader says that there are only two times that people might really *do nothing* to deal with a bad work situation and that *doing nothing* might be the best option. These times are when either your boss is leaving the job or you will shortly be leaving.

C. Participants are divided into four groups. Each group is asked to stand in front of one of the sheets of newsprint. One member in each group will be designated the scribe. Their responsibility will be to write under each heading the comments from fellow group members. Each group is asked to brainstorm reasons why each "do nothing" heading may be an ineffective thing to do.

D. Each group gets 5-10 minutes at each topic and then rotates to the next one until all groups have moved around the room writing their comments on each sheet of newsprint.

E. Discuss the comments in the large group.

Group Discussion:

- To help clarify any confusion about what each topic means, the group leader can use the following information as a guideline for group discussion:

✓ *Complaining:*	"Many times employees spend a lot of time complaining about their problem bosses to other people who aren't really in a position to do anything about the problem, like co-workers, friends, and parents."
✓ *Keeping the Problem Inside:*	"These people do not share their problems with others. They hold it all in and let it eat away at them. Sometimes they begin to believe that they deserve it."

| ✓ *Doesn't Work Hard:* | "This is probably the most common form of *doing nothing*. Symptoms of this behavior include coming in late for work, waiting to be told what to do instead of taking initiative, and just plain goofing off." |
| ✓ *Escaping:* | "This could include using alcohol or drugs to forget your problems. Also watching a lot of television or staying indoors all weekend to escape the outer world." |

- This exercises uses the cooperative teaching technique called "Carousal Brainstorming" which is effective with all age groups. Brainstorming is allowing participants to express the first idea or thought that comes to mind without the fear of being judged right or wrong.
- This exercise works well with preteen and teenage groups.

Registering a Complaint

Purpose:

    1. To use language appropriate to the context.
    2. To practice communication appropriate to people in the context (e.g., age, sex, etc.).
    3. To improve interpersonal relationship skills.

Materials:

Situation cards written on index cards; tape recorder; poster board or other large writing surface; markers.

Description:

    A. The group sits in a large circle leaving one end open for role playing. Each group member will take turns choosing a situation card and reading it out loud for the group to understand.
    B. The participant will then pick a partner to role play the situation, or a role play partner will be designated by the group leader. Each role play will be recorded.
    C. Following each role play, the leader replays the tape and has the participants analyze the language used as well as the effectiveness/appropriateness of their communication.
    D. The leader will make an outline on the poster board of the group members' comments relating to the stated objectives of the exercise.

Group Discussion:

- The situation cards should have short scenarios in which a complaint needs to be made with a store clerk, restaurant manager, teacher, and so on. Sample situations include the following:

    ✓ The food you ordered in a restaurant was served cold.
    ✓ You've been sitting in a restaurant for 20 minutes and no one served you.
    ✓ You are returning a packaged shirt you bought that had a torn collar.
    ✓ Your teacher accused you unjustly of writing graffiti in a textbook found on your desk. You're going to discuss the matter with the teacher after school.
    ✓ A clerk in a department store refused to help you find something because he was "too busy."

- This exercise works well with all age groups at any stage of group development.

One-Way Talking

Purpose:

    1. To illustrate the importance of two-way communication.
    2. To practice giving directions and asking questions.

Materials:

    Paper; "One-Way Talking Picture Cards;" writing materials.

Description:

    A. The group leader begins by explaining that one-way talking involves one person speaking; the other person cannot ask questions or make any comments. Each participant is given paper to draw on and writing materials.
    B. The leader asks for a volunteer to describe a picture for the class to draw using one of the "One-Way Talking Picture Cards."
    C. The group members are reminded that they cannot speak in any way (i.e., cannot ask questions or ask for something to be repeated). When finished, group members are asked to show their pictures to each other. Do they come close to matching the picture card?
    D. Discuss why one-way talking is an *ineffective* method of communication.
    E. Repeat the activity using two-way talking and compare the pictures to the original being described. Discuss the results.

Group Discussion:

- When discussing why one-way talking is ineffective, ask members how they felt during the first activity opposed to the second one in which they could ask questions and make comments.
- Discuss times when participants felt they were being "talked at" rather than "talked to." How did they feel and react in those situations? Do they ever "talk at" other people? Why? Are they aware of it?
- This is a fun exercise that can be used effectively with older children with a variety of communication and behavioral needs.

One-Way Talking Picture Cards

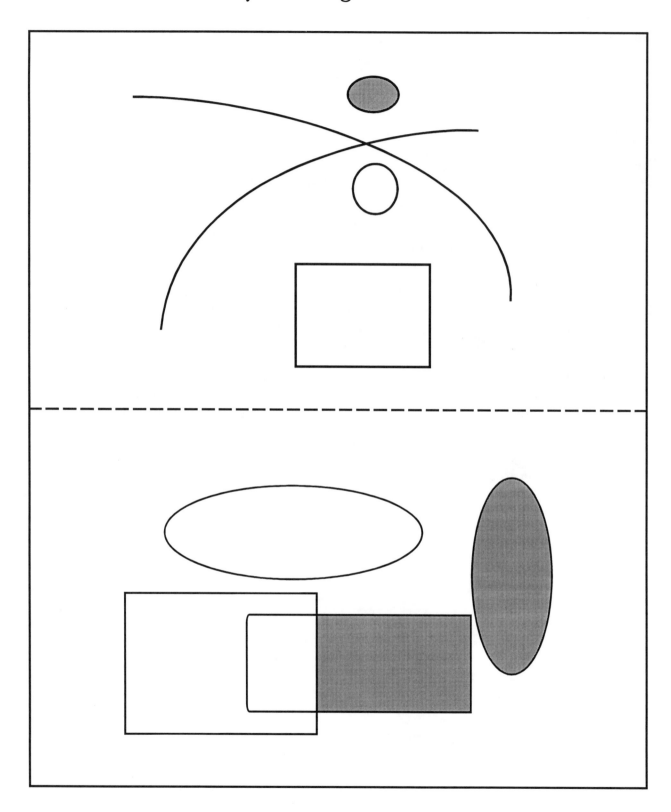

Follow Your Intuition

Purpose:

1. To increase self-awareness.
2. To develop group cohesiveness.

Materials:

None

Description:

A. The group leader begins this exercise by asking group members if anyone has ever had the experience of thinking about a friend and the next day the friend calls on the telephone or you receive a letter in the mail (or on E- mail). Discuss responses. The leader suggests that one way to explain this occurrence is by understanding a very useful part of our mind's thought process that is called your intuition.

B. The leader explains that this exercise will test how well someone's intuition is working. Five volunteers are asked to stand shoulder to shoulder in a straight line in front of the group. The participants are asked to close their eyes and imagine that they are a *solid* brick wall. One designated person in line will imagine that they are "air" as opposed to solid brick. Concentration is important for success in this exercise.

C. The group leader asks for another volunteer who will test his or her intuition. This participant will walk around the line of five people four times while also thinking "air." After the fourth time circling the group, he or she slowly walks into the person who is also thinking "air." If that person is air, he or she will move out of the way. The participant walking around the line will first be asked to wait outside of the room while the person in line who is "air" is chosen.

D. Discuss results and repeat the exercise with different volunteers.

Group Discussion:

- When discussing the meaning of intuition, the leader explains that intuition is a different thought process than using one's intellect or trying to "figure something out." The understanding or knowledge just comes to you without any effort or understanding about how it came. For example, some people understand how to play music intuitively without ever taking a music lesson; others can know the answer to a math problem without really trying to solve it. Intuition is in a different realm than the intellect. Being intuitive is not the same as being psychic.

- Discuss ways in which one can use intuition in everyday life (e.g., knowing when not to walk down a certain street due to possible danger; knowing when to take advantage of an opportunity; understanding and trusting yourself when it comes to developing relationships).

- This is a fun exercise that can have thought-provoking results. It is most successful with groups that have established some degree of trust and group rapport.

Our Community

Purpose:

1. To provide an opportunity for community involvement.
2. To increase group cohesiveness and positive interdependence.

Materials:

One copy of the "Improving Our Community" activity sheet for each group; writing materials.

Description:

A. The group members are asked to sit in a large circle. Each member is asked to briefly talk about their community likes, dislikes, and areas that need to be improved.
B. The group leader divides the group into triads and gives each group one activity sheet to complete. After 15-20 minutes each group chooses a spokesperson to share community improvement ideas with the large group.
C. The leader facilitates a discussion around how to actualize their community improvement plans.

Group Discussion:

- The group discussion should focus on two main goals that have to do with examining ways to function within a community: (a) improving the community's physical areas and (b) how to make the improvement plans work. Groups might decide to work together on a weekend toward a mutually agreed-upon project.
- Some of the ideas generated for improving one's community can include the following:

  ✓ Organizing a clean-up day at the local park
  ✓ Developing a bike trail
  ✓ Having a town farmer's market on weekends
  ✓ Planting flowers

- This activity can be a powerful tool for helping group members develop the social skills needed in being able to work together toward a greater goal.
- This exercise can work well with a variety of age groups at different stages of development.

Improving Our Community

Directions: Working together to improve your community is a worthwhile task and can be a lot of fun. With the members of your group, discuss and write answers to the following questions:

(1) What are some areas of your community that you think need improving?

(2) How would you begin making these improvements?

(1) AREAS THAT NEED IMPROVEMENT

1. **Example:** The school playground is real messy with litter and trash. _____

2. _____

3. _____

4. _____

5. _____

(2) IMPROVEMENT PLAN

What is needed for taking the first step toward making that improvement?

1. **Example:** Contact the school principal and decide on a date and time for the clean-up. _____

2. _____

3. _____

4. _____

5. _____

Please visit us online at:

http://www.prpress.com

This website contains:

- ✓ Descriptions of all of our titles with
  - complete tables of contents
  - reviews of our books
  - author biographies
- ✓ Online ordering
- ✓ Online queries and requests for catalogs
- ✓ Information on our home-study continuing education programs
- ✓ Our publishing guidelines
- ✓ The history of our company

. . . . and much, much more!

Catalog Request

For our latest catalog and ordering information, please write, call, fax, or e-mail the following information:

Name: _____
PLEASE PRINT CLEARLY

Address (Company name if business address): _____

_____

Address: _____

City/State/Zip: _____ Country: _____

Phone Number: _____

I am a (check one):
- ☐ Psychologist   ☐ School Psychologist
- ☐ Clinical Social Worker   ☐ Psychiatrist
- ☐ Marriage and Family Therapist   ☐ Other: _____
- ☐ Mental Health Counselor

Please send this form to:

Professional Resource Press, P.O. Box 15560, Sarasota, FL 34277-1560.
You can also contact us by phone (1-800-443-3364), FAX (1-941-343-9201),
or e-mail (orders@prpress.com).